Daniel Martin

FROM WHITEBOARDS TO WEB 2.0

Activating language skills with new technologies

HELBLING LANGUAGES

From Whiteboards to Web 2.0
by Daniel Martin
© HELBLING LANGUAGES 2015

First published 2015
ISBN 978-3-85272-939-8

Edited by Thomas Strasser
Copy edited by Jill Florent
Designed by Giorgia Probani
Cover design by Capolinea
Printed by Bieffe

Contents

Contents

Contents

Introduction

This book is aimed at secondary/higher education/adult English teachers interested in enhancing their teaching with technology. Some of you may have IWBs, some may have a computer and a projector, and others may encourage your learners to bring their own Internet connecting devices to class. The book is suitable for both the tech-savvy and for the novice because these three principles have been applied: a) the activities do not require much preparation time (and in many cases none at all); b) the suggested Web tools are user-friendly; and c) methodology, cognitive engagement and interaction in the target language takes priority over the technical side of things.

Using this book

You will find a wide array of activities for all language levels that suggest using various technologies that you may have at your disposal. You may want to choose an activity and follow the steps in the suggested exploitation. However, my suggestion is to look for activities that can fit in well with a given topic, language area or language skill that you are currently working on with your students and blend them in with your own vision and ideas as well as with other materials that you would like to use in class.

An estimated time for completion of the activities is given. However, feel free and be ready to adapt the step-by-step procedure to your teaching style, time availability, or your learners' needs and interests. It is always possible to skip some of those steps or to augment the content, thus decreasing or increasing the amount of time required.

All activities include at least two variations and a follow-up that extends the activity outside the classroom. The main activity and the variations do not exclusively involve using IWB/whiteboard software and Web 2.0 tools. A strong emphasis has been placed on integrating technology in the classroom with other scenarios where students have to use the language creatively through speaking and writing (with pen and paper).

Visit **www.helblinglanguages.com/fromwhiteboards**

to find video tutorials on how to use some of the Web 2.0 tools included in the book. There are two short video tutorials (also known as screencasts or videocasts) for each tool.

The first video tutorial focuses on the technical side of things, it guides you through aspects like the registration process (if needed), what the tool does and how to use it. You can, however, delve deeper into the technicalities and explore more by taking the initiative of running your own searches on the Internet. For instance, if the tool in question is Wordle, you can type the keywords "wordle tutorial" into the search box in Google and have a look at the list of websites. For better results, click on Advanced Search and then refine your search by using the date and file type options. It is a good idea to select Web pages updated in the last year, because the tutorials will contemplate the latest versions and features. You may also select Adobe Acrobat PDF, Microsoft Word or Microsoft Powerpoint from the file type menu. I also highly recommend running the same search on YouTube for other video tutorials. You may also find tutorials for many Web tools referenced in this book at

Introduction

www.helblinglanguages.com/mindtheapp/, which hosts screencasts for Web tools referenced in Thomas Strasser's book Mind the App.

The second tutorial centers on didactics and shows you the tool from an English teaching angle. Quite interestingly, the most popular, and effective, Internet sites and Web 2.0 tools used by language teachers are not intrinsically language learning ones. For example, networking sites, video and audio recorders, mindmapping or videoconferencing tools, turn out to be excellent media for language practice and interaction, creation of content, channelling teacher's feedback and bonding. You will find in this type of tutorial practical ideas and insights into how you and your learners can benefit from the integration of these tools into language learning both inside and outside the classroom.

Finally, the quick-reference guide at the back allows you to search activities by language focus, language level, estimated running time, and type of tools.

Using new technologies

Teachers and learners have always made use of technology. Even, pen and paper or the chalkboard were new technologies once upon a time. We no longer think of them as technologies because they are normalized now, in the same sense as computers are second nature in the workplace for many sectors. Some twentieth-century technologies have become or are in the process of becoming obsolete. Language labs are losing ground in favour of class sets of laptops or tablets or of learners bringing their own devices. Overhead projectors are being replaced by computers and data projectors, which are more versatile tools.

There are various factors that contribute towards the democratization and normalization of a given technology. Some of the most important are ease of use, affordability, the capability of doing old things in new ways and, especially, the capability of doing new things in new ways. A prime example of a normalized technology is the smartphone: it is true that prices have increased as phones have become more sophisticated and powerful, nevertheless, the average phone is an affordable tool. Old things (talking and texting) can be done in new ways (through videocalls or using online networking sites). In addition, new things can be done in new ways (using the phone as a computer that we can carry in our pockets). Although these factors are essential for the normalization of any technology in the classroom environment, the most important factor is pedagogy.

Firstly, as a teacher you need a good reason to choose to integrate one tool rather than another, or no tool at all, in your lesson. For example, Twitter (an online social networking and microblogging site that allows users to send and read "tweets", or short messages, limited to 140 characters) can be a very useful medium for microwriting. Learners can drill language chunks independently outside class hours and then their tweets can be accessed from the whiteboard next time you see the class. You can thus praise good use of language in plenary mode as well as providing recycling and extra exposure. Alternatively, you may decide to give your learners a few minutes of class time to write tweets using pen and paper. In that case, the learners are immediately on task and the use of class time is maximized. While learners are working, you can circulate and provide help as needed. Then, when the learners get home, they can access the Internet from their smartphones, laptops or tablets and type on Twitter what they wrote in class.

Secondly, in addition to the technical competence required, learners also need to think digitally. Thinking digitally encompasses a wide range of issues, such as making fair use of digital media, being aware of the potential risks of projecting oneself online, having an open mind to work collaboratively in social frameworks and especially taking a critical look at a given technology or gadget to evaluate how it could be exploited for language learning.

Taking the same example of Twitter above, you can embrace it from a teaching angle and use it as a lexical tool. By running searches on Twitter with double inverted commas around language chunks you can instantly obtain very relevant examples of authentic language. You can thus create opportunities for microreading or, in other words, engage the learners in intensive reading by exposing them to multiple and very short texts containing tailor made language chunks. When you know what is beyond a technology and are acquainted with the potential to use it for microreading and vocabulary practice you can foster learner autonomy by encouraging your learners to benefit from it outside the classroom.

It follows that the terms "digital natives" (people who were born with the digital technologies) and "digital immigrants" (people who were not and who at some stage in their lives have adopted these technologies), coined by Marc Prensky (2001), or seemingly young kids versus older people, may no longer (if they ever did) bear relation to reality. For one thing, the stereotypical nature of these terms underestimates the potential for thinking outside the box and finding other uses of a given technology, tool or gadget to suit our needs as language teachers. In addition, this generalization does not account for the fact that, with the abundance of Web tools or apps, comes specialization. It is not age that determines level of mastery but rather frequency of use and repeated actions. Most teachers will know how to operate copy machines better than the students they teach by the simple fact that they get to use them whereas the students most likely do not. Younger generations are very dexterous at texting from their phones by force of habit but the degree of cognitive depth of those information exchanges is also an active agent in an effective use of this technology.

Taking risks and embracing new challenges is inherent to teaching and that involves trying out new tools. It is understandable that sometimes you may feel out of your comfort zone because of uncertainty of educational outcomes or lack of technical expertise. If that is the case, it is important to take small steps. In other words, you should focus on certain aspects of one given tool or technology which you believe will facilitate learning. Once you are familiar with integrating that tool, you can feel more encouraged and at ease in introducing and integrating other tools. It is, again, fundamental to bear in mind that, even though there may well be teachers and students who are more knowledgeable on the technical side of things and have a higher rate of speed when doing things digitally, if you have a clear understanding of the pedagogic purpose of a technology in use, you are likely to put it into practice competently and effectively.

At the other end of the spectrum, you should not get overexcited and use technology indiscriminately believing that it offers the ultimate answer. There is no doubt at this stage about the positive impact of technology in education and therefore the need to integrate it when it is available: whether it is outside the confines of the classroom with mobile technologies and virtual learning environments or in the classroom setting with Internet connected devices, interactive whiteboards, a data projector and a screen or a combination of what is available to us. However, using or (worse still) overusing technology because of its allure, because it is there or because that is what our learners expect are not good enough reasons. The use of technology needs to take place in a principled way.

Important considerations when using the Internet

Copyright

Many images, songs and videos on the Internet are copyright protected. When using them as a resource, do abide by fair use and observe applicable copyright regulations. When searching for images on Google, for instance, you may click on the Advanced Search options button and then choose "free to use or share" from "usage rights" on the menu. Another good source for images is the image hosting site Flickr. You may look for pictures under Creative Commons Licence there.

Plagiarism

Learners need to know that they should credit original sources when using someone else's work. They may use small parts of a work, such as a quotation of a sentence or a paragraph as long as credit is given. And, obviously, they should never pass off someone else's work taken from the Internet as their own.

Permission

Some activities in this book suggest using personal photos, recording videos or holding videoconferences. If you are teaching underage students, you will have to get their parents'/guardians' permission, stating and ensuring that this digital material will only be used for educational purposes within the classroom environment.

Safety

Many websites require registration and a valid email account must be provided. It is highly recommended to have a secondary email account to sign-up for new sites and use a strong password that includes special characters, numbers and/or upper and lower case letters. Log in information should not be shared.

Digital footprint

Everything we do online leaves a footprint that, like tattoos, cannot be removed (or may be very difficult to do so). This is particularly important when we upload personal videos or photos to social networking sites, as these can be shared by third parties and then control over who sees them and, in turn, shares them is relinquished. Employers, for instance, may check out candidates' postings as a screening device.

CHAPTER 1
INTERACTIVE WHITEBOARDS AND WHITEBOARDS

Chapter 1

What are interactive whiteboards (IWBs)?

The first mental picture that the term "interactive whiteboards" (IWBs) conjures up is one of a whiteboard mounted on a wall at the front of the classroom with a projector on top or on the ceiling and connected to a computer. However, this is not the only kind of interactive whiteboard. Laptops, tablets and smartphones, can be interactive whiteboards as well because they are computers we can interact with by tapping on what is displayed on the screen. The next development will be a proliferation of other "smart" portable devices such as smartwatches, whose functions go beyond those of timekeeping and are similar to those of a smartphone worn on the wrist. Likewise, smartglasses, which are non prescription glasses with a digital display directly in front of the wearer's field of vision. These glasses enable an overlay of virtual environments. A doctor, for instance, can perform an operation while seeing an MRI scan overlaid on a patient. The most obvious difference among the devices mentioned above is the size. We could say that a tablet, for instance, is a small interactive whiteboard. We can use it to surf the Web, create content, watch videos, play music or open files by tapping with our fingers on the screen. Or we could say that an interactive whiteboard is a big tablet that allows us to perform the same actions.

What are the advantages and disadvantages of different types of IWB?

The most fundamental issue is not what these devices can do but rather what we want to achieve. Smaller screens on light mobile devices are ideal for individual use and for learners to work at their own pace in class or on the move. Bigger screens are adequate for plenary teaching and they provide a large and common viewing area and working space to engage a group of learners. In practical terms, the students might be using their mobile phones, tablets or laptops independently in class or outside class to do some vocabulary-related exercises from a website or to play a vocabulary game at various difficulty levels. Then teachers can devise scenarios, either with or without technology, for the students to use the vocabulary. Twitter is a great resource for working with lexis. Searches for tweets containing specific words or phrases can also be made by users. If there is an IWB in the classroom, you could, for instance, as part of the lesson preparation, take a look at the target vocabulary, type those words up on Twitter, take screenshots of tweets containing those words, paste the resulting pictures on different pages of a document and finally place blotches of ink over those words. In class, you can project the pictures on the board and invite the students to look at the screen in order to guess what the missing words might be first in pairs, then in plenary mode. Next you can invite a student to come up to the front and use the eraser to reveal the hidden words, then ask the class to generate sentences that are true of themselves using those words. You could also access an online concordancer to take a look on the board and see how those target words combine with other words and delve into further uses. Finally, you may ask the students to go back to their laptops or tablets again in class or outside class to post some entries on a class blog or wiki for some individual or collaborative writing practice with the target vocabulary. Next day the lesson can be started by having a look on the IWB at the students' writing samples to review the vocabulary. In the examples above the things that can be done on laptops, tablets or the IWB are the same but if you want to achieve full cognitive and social engagement you have to establish beforehand which course of action is more suitable for your chosen tool.

What cheaper alternatives to IWBs are there?

Concerns have been raised regarding the cost of equipping classrooms with IWBs. Is this cost effective? Should the money, if available at all, be spent more wisely on other technologies? Here are three cheaper alternatives to IWBs that might be worth having in mind as well.

Infrared and ultrasound receivers are attached to the edge of a whiteboard and transform it into an interactive whiteboard. A software programme is installed in the computer and the whiteboard is calibrated with a stylus. The main advantage, besides the more affordable price, is that they can be transported and used in different rooms. The downside is the need for set up and calibration each time they're moved. The two most popular brands are Ebeam (www.e-beam.com) and Mimio (www.mimio.com). Each brand comes with a companion software to create lessons and to perform actions on the board such as writing, creating objects, typing text, placing and dragging images, etc.

Remote Desktop Apps are downloadable apps that wirelessly connect a mobile device (tablet or iPad) to a main computer so that users may control the computer from the device. A software programme is installed in the main computer and an app is installed in the mobile device. This allows you to walk around the class while holding the mobile device and to write and display content on the whiteboard from anywhere in the room. Splashtop (www.splashtop.com) can be downloaded to all devices (free at the time of writing) and Doceri (www.doceri.com) is an app for iPad (single license at the time of writing was $30.00).

Wireless networking is possible with some data projectors. A connection via Bluetooth between the projector and a mobile device can be set up, once again allowing for mobility in the classroom. An alternative to wireless networking is a mobile device connected to the projector with an HDMI cable. In this instance you will be restricted to standing or sitting at the front facing the students.

Plain whiteboards can be combined with a computer, a data projector and cable or/and wireless Internet connection. Many educators and institutions decide to use this combination as a cheaper alternative to interactive whiteboards. With the same budget a greater number of rooms can be equipped with this set up rather than with interactive whiteboards and therefore a greater number of teachers and students can benefit from it on a regular basis so that integration of technology becomes part of the regular fabric of classroom life. In addition, many educators believe that although it is practical and enjoyable to be able to do things on the IWB such as annotating words, drawing, dragging objects, playing videos or browsing the Web, the true interaction lies in the cognitive and emotional engagement with the content provided by teachers or students to meet educational outcomes and this can be achieved equally well with a plain whiteboard. Not being able to control the computer from the board itself but having to use the keyboard or mouse of the computer may not, therefore, be such a crucial factor.

How can you use a Whiteboard to promote interaction?

Asking a student to come to the front of the classroom to drag things on the big screen with his finger or a stylus or to tap on an icon while the rest of the students are passively looking at the board are not highly interactive activities. In the best of cases, this might be interactive for the student in front but that is not an optimal teaching situation. However, by asking a student to perform the same actions while engaging everyone else by posing questions or asking the students to react to the actions performed at the front, you are generating interaction in the classroom. It may be telling the students to stand up if they like or enjoy doing something conveyed by a given word or language chunk that you have just displayed on the board. You might make a few short voice recordings with controversial statements (e.g. *We are too dependent on computers and smart phones. We have forgotten how to socialize with each other*) and then embed them on a slide, ask a student to come to the front and tap on an audio icon for the rest of the students to listen and look for a partner who agrees or disagrees with a given statement, have a thirty-second conversation about it, then ask a few students to share out their feelings in plenary mode. It is this interaction of the student with the content on the board together with the full cognitive and perhaps also physical engagement of the rest of the class and of your involvement as a teacher to activate learning, that determine the interactive nature of these actions.

As expressed earlier, a set up of a whiteboard, computer and data projector could equally engage the whole class of students in these examples of interactions. The student in the front would then have to use the computer keyboard and/or mouse instead of dragging things or tapping on icons on the board but, in essence, the learning outcomes would not be undermined.

Do Whiteboards lead to frontal teaching?

Critics of IWBs suggest that their use reduces interaction in the classroom by encouraging frontal lecture-mode teaching where the teacher speaks and the students, reduced to a spectator role, listen. This means that students have fewer opportunities for hands-on experience and learning by doing. I have personally witnessed many lessons where this is very much the case as boards are overused but there are many examples of both outstanding and mediocre teaching practices with and without technology. In my view, an effective use of the board entails taking a look at this technology and other technologies at our disposal or at our students' disposal, and deciding, as in the examples above, what we want to do and how best to achieve it. The board is just a tool and should be used sparingly at the right times and in combination and interaction with other tools, materials and most importantly, because this is when it becomes truly interactive, with the students' minds. Although far from being an advocate for frontal teaching, I still believe that there are certain times when frontal teaching, in small doses, is required and beneficial. Sharing a personal anecdote or telling a joke or a short story to illustrate grammar points or to expose learners to relevant lexis are all examples of engaging frontal teaching without technology. The board can boost teaching, if used reasonably, as it is in fact a hub for many useful digital tools and resources. The board allows you to access content placed on the Web or content that you or your students create. You can prepare materials, interact with them, make modifications and save them again for future use. You can play and record videos, audios, use digital versions of textbooks, reach out to the world and have online meetings with other groups of students, look for images to illustrate things or to spark off discussions and present things in visually appealing ways. Not all of these actions will fall under the consideration of frontal teaching but, even when that is the case, when used in moderation and in combination with other actions, they do make perfect pedagogical sense.

Whiteboards as digital hubs

The IWB (or the whiteboard computer and a projector set-up) is a very powerful tool incorporating many other tools of great relevance for the language classroom. You can load a digital version of the textbook to the main computer and play audio and video recordings by simply clicking on the icons displayed on the pages. You can also zoom in to enlarge parts of a page, such as those showing images, for heads-up teaching and interaction and annotate (or type) and save relevant vocabulary or Internet links on those pages.

In addition to digital textbooks, you can also benefit from many other digital resources such as CD-Roms with vocabulary and grammar activities for the class or supplementary material from the Internet to enrich lessons. This material may be available for purchase or free of cost from ELT publishing companies. There are also many other resources to be found on the Internet such as those providing grammar- or vocabulary-based content as well as interactive games, dictionaries, encyclopedias, videos, lexical tools or language apps that you can bring to class from the whiteboard. Some are specifically designed for English teaching and learning purposes and others, while designed for other purposes, nevertheless provide great engaging content for language learning.

Whiteboard companion softwares, (see page 29), are also very interesting tools that provide different sorts of stimuli. You can combine images, videos and typed text and save the material in a pen drive, then have it ready to use in class, thus maximizing teaching time.

Whiteboards are in fact bearers of media and facilitate access to a wide range of tools that in many cases were already available but in many different physical forms, whereas now they are integrated into one single piece of equipment. Whiteboards are chalkboards, overhead projectors, audio and video players, audio and video recorders, videoconferencing tools, cameras, Internet browsers and, last but not least, bearers of Web 2.0 tools.

How does using a Whiteboard change the teacher's role?

The teacher can become a DJ because the convergence of tools and pieces of equipment creates many exciting opportunities to combine different types of visual and auditory stimuli at the click of a mouse or at the tap of a screen. It is therefore tempting to get overexcited with this wealth of technology-driven materials, which may actually lead to impoverishing your lessons by neglecting other types of technology-free materials and activities. A sense of purpose and a critical look at what you bring into the classroom, with and without technology, needs to be borne in mind. At any rate, you can prepare materials beforehand, bring them to the classroom and have them on cue ready to be used in due course.

For instance, you may decide to work on two pages from a digital textbook and have the pages ready on the screen, then click on the Internet browser and open five tabs (one with a video from YouTube which has been paused and which will be played at a later time, another one with an online dictionary, a third tab with a pronouncing dictionary, a fourth tab with Google homepage to run a search for pictures to clarify meaning of words that are best explained visually, and a fifth one with an online voice recording application for students to make recordings on in class). In addition, you may have created an activity for the class using a companion software, which has been saved in a memory stick to be opened on the computer for later use.

Prior to meeting the students, you have a mental script of the various activities that will take place in class and of how the technology available to you can facilitate learning. The resources deployed in the example above are manifestations of planned interactions of technology-enhanced lessons. Equally interesting are the many other spontaneous interactions that may occur as well, because teaching also necessitates handling unpredictability. Incorporating technology into teaching is both a skill and an art requiring having to juggle between a deliberate playlist of media and giving room for other technology-driven stimuli brought out by the uncertainties of teaching as it happens.

The Web is an invaluable source for exposure to English. Content generated in English is increasing all the time and the Web's reach is spreading fast. In practical terms, more and more learning centres and classrooms are being equipped with Internet connections and IWBs or whiteboards. Educators can go online and access the wealth of resources at the push of a button. Even when there is no Internet provision in the school or classroom, you can always look for material beforehand, save it and bring it to class. In addition, more and more learners have their own Internet connecting devices such as mobile phones, laptops or tablets, which can be used in class and outside it for language learning purposes.

CHAPTER 2
WEB 2.0

Chapter 2

Web 1.0 and Web 2.0

The term Web 2.0 implies that there was an earlier version of the Web, or Web 1.0. If so, what are Web 1.0 and Web 2.0? How are they different? In which ways is Web 2.0 an improved version of its predecessor?

From the early days of the Internet up until about 2004 the Web 1.0 was a place where users mostly accessed information. Whether it was newspapers, encyclopedias, train timetables or shopping, things moved in one direction: content was placed on the Web for people to read or buy. There was hardly any interaction other than email exchanges and text or voice instant messaging. Content creators were for the most part webmasters whose role was to update sites and little room was left for users to interact with the uploaded material. In addition, visually appealing design was undermined by slow Internet connections. Many users could not stream videos and a considerable number of images on a page implied a longer waiting time for it to load. This meant that webmasters often decided to display mostly text and keep visual content to a bare minimum. There was no reason for visitors to return regularly to a given site, as content was static.

In contrast, Web 2.0, gives a richer experience and a more inclusive space which offers people tools to create, share and interact with content. Facebook, founded in 2004, is essentially a blank slate brought to life by mass participation from users who post messages, photos and videos and interact with each other. Other examples of the dynamic nature of this interactive Web are Flickr (2004), YouTube (2005) and Twitter (2006). Faster connections and smaller devices have resulted in people not merely clicking on a link to read an article or on a shopping cart icon to buy goods but also grabbing their mobile phones and taking photos or videos of current events and uploading them on social networking sites. In this way, Web users are providing real-time reporting of news as it unfolds to a wide audience. This is an authentic example from a Twitter account: http://twitpic.com/135xa. *There's a plane in the Hudson. I'm on the ferry going to pick up the people. Crazy.* In Web 1.0 users accessed online newspapers to read news. In Web 2.0 this still applies but things do not move in a one-way direction. It may well be the case that newspapers access users' Twitter, Facebook or YouTube accounts to look for photos and videos which they will, in turn, supply to their readers.

Using Web 2.0 online tools

Web 2.0 is also distinguished by its range of online tools. It is no longer necessary to install CDs or download software programmes in order to create, edit and share content made up of images, audio recordings, videos and text. Many of these tools have a free of cost version and a paid version with extra features. In many instances registration is not needed, so the tool can be used right away by simply accessing the Web address. Web 2.0 permits learners to create material and to interact with it. They can work collaboratively or independently, in class or elsewhere,. A unique Web address is generated for each media presentation, word cloud, video, voice recording, virtual notice board, screencast, etc. This is highly convenient for the language classroom as teachers and learners can easily share content via emails or by providing the link or, in many instances, by embedding it onto a blog, wiki or networking site.

Chapter 2

Having an IWB/whiteboard in the classroom means that all this work can be accessed right away and at ease from the front and you can devise teaching scenarios for learners to interact with it.

Invisible technology

When a technology has become normalized, that is, when it has been used significantly, naturally and purposefully over a stretch of time, we are no longer consciously aware of it as a technology: it becomes an invisible enabler. Examples of normalized or invisible technologies are the car or the television. It is true that things do not move at the same pace for everyone as far as Web 2.0 tools are concerned. What is second nature for some may not be a normalized use of technology for others yet but Web 2.0 is having an increased impact on our everyday lives and on the way we relate to others. Taking a picture with a mobile phone and uploading to a social networking site such as Facebook or sharing it via an instant messaging service such as WhatsApp is for many as natural and mechanical as turning the TV on or starting up the car.

Web 2.0 tools are fairly intuitive and easy to use. Obviously some tools are more sophisticated than others and the degree of digital competency of users will vary. In any case, many activities with a high degree of cognitive depth can be devised and great outcomes can be achieved by means of frills-free tools. A prime example of this is the voice recorder Vocaroo (www.vocaroo.com). All that is required is a click on the red button for learners to put the language to practice. Another good example is the word cloud generator Wordle (www.wordle.net). We are presented with a text box for typing or copying and pasting text for the tool to generate a poster with words. In truth, the most difficult thing about using Web 2.0 tools is not knowing how to use them but having a clear focus and an end result in mind.

Language learning with Web 2.0

Web 2.0 tools are not language tools per se and neither are mobile devices. Many useful websites for the ELT classroom favoured by English teachers were not originally designed for English teaching purposes. However, if we bend them to our will, they can become incredibly powerful vehicles for exposure, creation, collaboration and interaction in the target language. This entails thinking outside the box on the part of the teacher. Take the digital notice board Padlet (www.padlet.com) for instance. Primarily, it is just a tool to keep notes and make announcements but it may be used in many different ways. Some ideas and activities are included in this book and in the videocasts suggesting how to use it for English language teaching and learning. Padlet can provide an excellent platform for students to keep an ongoing personal portfolio. They can use it to keep evidence of work or skills they have mastered either by embedding this work or by providing online links to it. It is also a great tool for students to do research and collaborate using computers, tablets or phones. You can also use it to assign homework: students write sentences using a given grammar structure or specific language chunks on the same virtual noticeboard. You can access their work in class from the IWB/whiteboard for revision and extra exposure. As Albert Einstein put it "imagination is more important than (technical) knowledge".

Chapter 2

Web 2.0 and collective intelligence

The concept of "harnessing collective intelligence" was coined by Tim O'Reilly (2005) to define Web 2.0. Many websites, such as YouTube or Wikipedia, owe their popularity to collective intelligence and synergy. Other websites, like Diigo or Flickr, have given rise to the new term "folksonomy", a system of classification made by regular people who use the Web. In the photo sharing website Flickr, for instance, users upload their personal pictures and "tag" them. In other words, they label them with key words so that pictures sharing common features can be searched and found under those key words or tags. Wikis are being embraced by many educators and are becoming key tools for students to produce work on both an individual and a team basis and to exchange learning experiences of various kinds. Wikis can be powerful tools for students to practise writing both individually and collaboratively as well as to edit other students' work. For example, students can practise the language they have learned through writing, they can also review what is being posted and edit each other's work or pool knowledge towards a common goal and write collaborative stories.

Web 2.0 and remix literacy

The term "remix" is mostly associated with music and it implies recreating preexisting songs to produce different versions. In a broader sense of the word, Lawrence Lessing (2005) posits that culture as a whole can be construed as a remix. The combined effect of a widespread use of the Internet and the popularity of appealing and highly intuitive online-based digital tools has resulted in a surge of new ways of generating, handling, transmitting and decoding meaning. As a result, literacy has been redefined. It is no longer limited to putting and interpreting thoughts on paper or on a screen through text but also encompasses creative use and remix of hybrid formats combining text, images, sounds and videos. Younger generations may have more natural talent and dexterity in handling these digital materials but as educators we should ensure that they use them as catalysts for critical thinking rather than producing superficial outcomes merely spotlighting alluring designs.

CHAPTER 3
FROM WHITEBOARDS TO WEB 2.0

Chapter 3

This book considers Whiteboards and Web 2.0 in a two-fold sense. Firstly, it contains activities for you to try out or to adapt in class that involve a combined use of Whiteboards (either IWBs or a whiteboard plus a computer and a data projector; whichever is your teaching situation) and Web 2.0 tools. Secondly, it reflects my personal journey from Whiteboards to Web 2.0. Although I still take advantage of the very helpful tools of IWB companion softwares, I find myself using Web 2.0 tools more and more (particularly so in combination with an IWB). It also makes pedagogical sense to embrace tools that learners already have with them on their phones, tablets or laptops and encourage them to use these tools both in class and outside the classroom environment.

Web 2.0 tools

In this section you will find the different types of Web 2.0 tools that are referenced in this book. There is a) a brief general description of what these tools do, b) a selection of activities contained in the book that suggest ways to use these tools and c) a list of websites where you can find them. The first tool listed in c) is the one I recommended using. Visit www.helblinglanguages.com/fromwhiteboardstoweb2.0 for video tutorials on how to use most of the first listed tool and for teaching ideas.

3.1 Word cloud generators

3.1 a Description
You can create word clouds by feeding some text into a text box to obtain a colourful poster featuring those words. Each word cloud has a unique URL so that it can be accessed online. A very interesting aspect is that the size of words in the resulting poster will be determined by their frequency in the typed or pasted text: the bigger the word; the more often it appeared in the text. You can print a word cloud, embed it onto a blog or wiki or take a snapshot of it and place it on a slide in Powerpoint or a page in your companion software.

3.1 b Activities
1.15 Proverbs, 3.1 A moment in time, 3.4 British English or American English?, 3.20 Shuffled letters, 3.26 Wrapping things up

3.1 c Suggested tools
- www.wordle.net
(the most popular word cloud generator among teachers)

- www.tagxedo.com
(will also post your word clouds to Facebook or Twitter)

- www.tagul.com (requires registration)

- www.wordsift.com (incorporates a visual thesaurus too)

- www.tagcrowd.com (lets you create PDFs of the word clouds)

- www.worditout.com
(you can save the word clouds by emailing them to yourself)

- www.abcya.com/word_clouds.htm
(highly recommended for primary education)

3.2 Videoconferencing

3.2 a Description

You can create a private videoconference in a few simple steps and the unique URL can be shared with a second or third party. Make sure you test the tool and share the URL before the students come to class. The advantage of using online videoconferencing tools rather than programs like Skype is that there is no need to download anything on either your computer or your speaking partner's computer.

3.2 b Activities

2.6 Countable or uncountable?, 2.25 Speaking exchange.
2.27 Translation exchange

3.2 c Suggested tools

- www.meetings.io (no registration required. It also includes many of the useful features found on Skype. In addition to videoconferencing you can also: engage in text chat, use a note pad and email, save and print the generated notes, share files, share the screen and go to full screen mode).

- www.sifonr.com (includes text chat, file share and embedding in websites, blogs or wikis)

- www.aol.com/av (frills free. Videoconferencing in two clicks)

- www.snapyap.com (requires registration)

- www.faceflow.com (requires registration)

- www.boostcam.com (includes text chat too)

- www.skype.com
(you need to download the programme and register to use it)

3.3 Video and audio recordings

3.3 a Description

You can make video recordings in the classroom in two ways: by using a camcorder, camera or mobile phone or by using online applications with your computer, tablet or mobile phone. The advantage of the former is that you have control over the recordings and you can edit them or delete them as you like. The main drawback is that the resulting files are usually too large to share, to email or to upload. The advantage of the latter is that online tools store those videos online and they can be accessed by typing (or copying and pasting) the unique Web address. The videos can be played right away or shared via a link. The main disadvantages are that those videos may eventually disappear or, if the unique URL is shared with third parties, you lose control over who watches the videos. Online video recorders are ideal for rehearsing and building up confidence in speaking and for students to create content and share with the class so that the resulting videos can be watched both in class and outside class. Simply go to the site, allow access to the camera, start recording and play back or share. Online audio recorders work in the same way.

3.3 b Activities
2.7 Fragmented listening, 2.8 Get it?, 2.9 Guest speaker, 2.12 Lips don't lie, 2.21 Ready for test

3.3 c Suggested tools
Video recordings

- www.mailvu.com (unlimited number of video recordings of up to 10 minutes of length each for the free version. Download the free app for the smartphone to record videos on the move)

- www.eyejot.com (requires registration. You can make a recording and email it. You can also save videos and download them to a computer)

- www.keek.com (social networking site to post videos and to reply to other users' videos)

- www.videomessageonline.com (record your video and share it with the generated URL. Videos are deleted after 30 days)

- http://frtr.me (records videos and posts them to Twitter)

Audio recordings

- www.vocaroo.com (a great tool. Record your voice and embed the recording to a website, or download it as mp3, email it, share the link, post the recording to social networking sites or create a qr code)

- www.recordmp3.org (click on the red button and download the recording as mp3 or share the link)

- www.audacity.sourceforge.net (open source software. It can record audio from multiple sources and features many editing options)

- www.audioboo.fm (enables you to post and share audiofiles)

3.4 Screencasting

3.4 a Description
A screencast (or video screen capture) is a video recording made by a computer of what's happening on the screen. Screencasts are very useful for tutorials on how to use computer programmes. There are many examples of video tutorials on YouTube, for instance. You can make screencasts with online applications or you can download software programmes. The suggested tools below are online applications.

3.4 b Activities
2.4 Bugging fly, 2.13 Literal video version, 2.17 One word at a time, 2.30 Voice artists

3.4 c Suggested tools
- www.screencast-o-matic.com (resize the frame to fit your recording area and record videos up to 15 minutes long and upload them to the site, to YouTube or download them as mp4, AVI or flash)

- www.screenr.com (record screencasts of up to five minutes and upload them you YouTube, embed them in a website or download them as mp4)

- www.screenbird.com (open source screencasting tool. Get the link to share or download the screencasts as mp4)

3.5 Text chat

3.5 a Description

Text chat is a good way to bring very fruitful language practice and interaction into the language classroom through a medium that many of our students identify with and are comfortable using. It can be used to provide writing practice in small but frequent doses and also to revisit lexis and ideas generated in class. If you retrieve the generated texts by copying and pasting them onto a word processing programme or by selecting a site that allows you to keep the private chat room active, you can display them on the board and devise activities for further consolidation. The creation of a private chat room for the class is a very quick and simple process.

3.5 b Activities

1.23 Texting, 2.18 Phone messages, 2.27 Translation exchange, 3.8 Find someone who, 3.18 Right a wrong

3.5 c Suggested tools

- www.todaysmeet.com (the main advantage of this site is that the chat room can remain active for up to a year. The generated texts can then be retrieved at a later time. It is also a good medium to post links of things of interest for the classroom or of online content created by the students for easier access)

- www.neatchat.com (includes a print option to print out the generated texts. It also has an upload files option)

- www.tinychat.com (in addition to text chat, users can also create live audio or video broadcasts)

- www.chatzy.com (you may also save or print a copy or create a virtual room for extra features)

3.6 Lexical tools

3.6 a Description

The first five tools below let us look in many different ways at how words are used not in isolation but in combination with other words. They are particularly useful for taking a critical look at word collocations and for exemplifying meanings and word usage. They are great resource tools to explore lexis and language chunks both in and outside class and then devise activities for the students to practise those words both in writing and speaking. The next five sites are dictionaries. Last but not least, Twitter, although obviously not a lexical tool, is included in this section because it can be used as one by running searches on it using inverted commas (as in "I wish I had", "cracking down on", "outrageously expensive" or "a far cry from"). The prompted results make great examples of natural use to have a look at on the board.

3.6 b Activities

2.10 How do you say it, 2.15 Minimal pairs, 3.6 Delving deeper, 3.17 Rhyming dictionaries, 3.19 Sound it, 3.23 Trending topics, 3.24 Vague language

3.6 c Suggested tools

- www.just-the-word (type a word in the search box and notice the different word combinations. The length of the green lines indicates the frequency of the combinations. Clicking on each prompted result will open up a list of examples from the British National Corpus).

- www.netspeak.org (use the symbols "...", "[ ]", "#" and "{}" in your searches to find more than one word, to compare options, to find similar words or check the order)

- www.phraseup.com (use the * to find missing words)

- www.phraseit.com (take a look at the example searches provided to learn the many different ways in which this tool can be used)

- www.fraze.it (take a look at the example searches provided to learn how to use the tool)

- www.wordreference.com
(very comprehensive dictionary. Visit the forums)

- www.wordnik.com
(multimedia dictionary including images and sounds)

- www.lingro.com
(copy and paste the URL onto the text box to make all the words on that page clickable and to get definitions when they are clicked on)

- www.howjsay.com (pronouncing dictionary. Type two or more words separated by semi-colon in the text box to create a word list)

- www.forvo.com (pronouncing dictionary featuring different varieties of English. Notice the download as mp3 link to download an audio recording of the word/s)

- www.twitter.com
(again, not a lexical tool per se but an invaluable site to get extremely good examples of language chunks and spoken grammar)

3.7 Blogs and wikis

3.7 a Description

Wikis (not to be confused with the most well known wiki, Wikipedia – which is an online encyclopedia that, unlike traditional encyclopedias, allows outside editing) or class blogs can be used to provide content, which can be easily accessed from the board. The students can also interact with blogs and wikis outside the classroom. For instance, you may place a short article in connection with a topic discussed in class for the students to send their comments in or you may embed a video played in class and ask the students to watch it again at home. Wikis are particularly interesting for collaborative work, especially in writing. The students may also create content using online tools, such as video or audio recordings or visual presentations, and embed the generated material in the class wiki or place the links for everyone to see both in and outside class.

3.7 b Activities
1.1 A thousand words is worth a picture, 2.14 Making comics, 2.25 Speaking exchange, 3.3 Bilingual blog, 3.25 Wikidictionary

3.7 c Suggested tools
Blogs

- www.wordpress.com (provides many very visually-appealing templates that make the blog look like a webpage, which is highly recommended if you want to set up a class blog).

- www.blogger.com
(presents more limited themes and design styles than Wordpress but it may be more useful for a student blog as opposed to a class blog).

- www.edublogs.org
(adequate for placing quizzes, handouts, assignments, etc.)

- www.tumblr.com (choose they type of post you want: image, text, video or link, and hit "publish")

- www.roon.io (very minimalist design. Ideal for diaries).

Wikis

- www.wikispaces.com (free for educators)

- www.pbworks.com (similar to wikispaces)

- www.sites.google.com (choose the classroom site template)

3.8 Mindmapping tools and online whiteboards

3.8 a Description
You can use mindmapping tools like virtual multimedia bulletin boards. Depending on the tool you decide to use you can type text, place pictures and embed audio recordings or videos on the bulletin board. You can also upload files, take pictures with a webcam or draw on them. You can create matching activities and then retrieve those documents in class. Students can create their own content and work individually or collaboratively and then show their work from the front on the board.
Online whiteboards share many of the features indicated above and may be used as a good alternative to interactive whiteboard softwares. Although they do not have the sophistication of most IWB softwares, they are perfectly functional for placing text, pen annotations, images and Internet links. In addition, most importantly, they are ideal for working collaboratively both synchronously and asynchronously, for sharing files and accessing the content generated either in class or outside.

3.8 b Activities
1.4 Conversation board game, 1.11 Myths and facts, 1.12 Our world, 2.29 Video board game, 3.12 *Luckily/Unluckily*

3.8 c Suggested tools
Mindmapping tools

- www.padlet.com (does not require registration. You can embed images and videos and open them in a enlarged screen within the created document)

- www.popplet.com (similar to padlet but requires registration. A nice feature is the pen tool, which is very convenient for interactive whiteboards)

- www.linoit.com (has the visual feel of a corkboard. Good for placing images and text)

- www.bubbl.us (adequate for brainstorming ideas collaboratively. It requires registration to save the generated content)

Online whiteboards

- www.twiddla.com (excellent alternative to interactive whiteboard softwares. Particularly useful if, in addition to typing or annotating words and expressions with the pen tool, you want to upload documents and then share the URL with the class)

- www.vyew.com (another great tool. The generated content can be exported as PDF)

- www.scriblink.com (features fewer options than twiddla or vyew but it is still a good alternative)

- www.awwapp.com (very minimalist whiteboard which offers just pen annotations. However, if that is the only thing you would like to do, it might be your first choice because it has more ample space to write on than the previous ones)

3.9 Annotation tools

3.9 a Description
Annotation tools (also known as bookmarking tools) enable you to underline, draw or highlight, type notes or take screen captures in webpages. You can access your annotations from other devices or share them with other people. There is an abundance of these tools on the Internet and most of them are extensions to browsers. By dragging a link onto the bookmarks bar of your browser or by downloading the extension (or add-on if you are using Firefox) then you can interact with the webpages as indicated above. All the tools below, with the exception of diigo, feature a pen tool that you can use to hide text from view.

3.9 b Activities
1.18 *Speak, spoke, spoken,* 3.22 The missing verb, 3.25 Wikidictionary

3.9 c Suggested tools
- www.awesomescreenshot.com (an extension that takes screen captures of full webpages or of selected areas. The blur tool is a good choice for hiding things from view. You can save the annotations as files or share them via a unique URL)

- www.drawhere.com (drag and drop the icon onto the bookmarks bar of your browser)

- www.bounceapp.com (enter the URL you want to annotate, add notes and share)

- www.scribblet.org (drag and drop the icon. Press "E" to send an email of the webpage with the annotations or copy and paste it)

- www.diigo.com (has a highlighter tool but does not feature the pen tool that is required for the activities above. One of the most popular and powerful bookmarking tools on the Internet)

3.10 Presentation tools

3.10 a Description
Online presentation tools share many of the features of familiar software programs such as PowerPoint for Windows or Keynote for Apple computers. You can place text, videos, audio recordings and images on pages or slides. The main advantage of using online tools is, once again, the ease of sharing and accessing documents either privately or publicly. Online tools also make collaborative work possible. There are many tools to choose from and your final choice should be determined by your needs or objectives.

3.10 b Activities
1.6 Five things, 1.7 From Italy to Brazil and back again, 1.11 Myths and facts, 1.22 Textbook writers

3.10 c Suggested tools
- www.voicethread.com (enables you to create slide-based presentations combining images, videos, text and recordings. Other users can interact with your presentations by typing their own comments or by placing voice recordings)

- www.prezi.com (similar to Powerpoint but instead of moving linearly, Prezi is based on paths within one page through which the presentation can travel)

- www.glogster.com (a "glog" or graphic blog is an interactive poster that can combine text, audio, video and images. Readers can interact with these posters)

- www.brainshark.com (allows you to upload images or a Word or Powerpoint document and then add voice narration by talking into a microphone. The resulting document can be shared via the unique URL or it can also be embedded in a webpage)

Whiteboard companion softwares

By installing a whiteboard companion software or a free open source software you can create your own teaching materials that can be saved, used, shared and adapted. These software programmes have many useful tools that allow you to place pictures, embed videos and audio files, type text, write annotations, place links to Internet sites or drag things on the board.
Each IWB brand comes with licensed companion software which you can install in the main computer connected to the board and also in your own computer so that activities can be created beforehand, saved in pen drives and then opened from the computer in the classroom.

Chapter 3

Licence policies vary but, broadly speaking, this software can be legally installed in a reasonable number of computers when an IWB (or a IWB receiver such as Mimio or Ebeam) is purchased.

Smartboard's software, Notebook, has two types of licences, a collaborative license (for use with interactive display devices) and a personal one (for personal computers that are associated with the purchase of an interactive product). The personal licence also permits Notebook software use with a non-interactive projector (in other words, a projector and a plain whiteboard). For more detailed information visit http://downloads01.smarttech.com/media/sitecore/en/pdf/legal/notebook-licensing-faq-public.pdf.

Promethean's software, Activinspire, features a personal edition and a professional edition. The first one is free of charge and users are permitted to use it with non-Promethean products. The professional edition is available free for Promethean board users or available to purchase for other board users or to use with a projector and a whiteboard. For more information and for download of the personal edition visit www.prometheanplanet.com.

Other IWB brands on the market that have their own companion software are Hitachi Starboard (http://eu.hitachi-solutions.com/en/index.php/), Sharp (http://sharp-world.com/products/iwb/), TeamBoard (www.teamboard.com), Panaboard (http://panasonic.net/pcc/eboard/interactive/), Polyvision (www.touchboards.com/polyvision/) and Interwrite (www.einstruction.com/products/interactive-whiteboards).

A very interesting alternative to commercial products like the ones indicated above is the free and open-source companion software Open-Sankoré, downloadable from www.open-sankore.org. It is highly recommended for those classrooms with a computer, projector and whiteboard set-up.

It does take some time to get familiar with using these companion softwares. However, an effective use does not lie so much in investing hours creating nicely designed lessons. On the contrary, it seems that the interaction of those software-based materials at specific moments with other technology-based and technology-free materials together with adequate teaching techniques is what brings satisfying learning experiences. For instance, you could simply choose to place a thought-provoking image on a blank page to stimulate discussion around a certain topic while providing useful lexis to engage learners. Then you could type conversation questions on another page for group work and speaking interaction. You could also ask the students to complete activities from their textbooks to reinforce the target language and then play a relevant video found on the Internet. Learners can also create their own digital content either in and outside the classroom, to be shared at a later time on the board. Useful as companion softwares are, they are not essential to learning outcomes.

CHAPTER 4 ACTIVITIES
4.1 IMAGE-BASED ACTIVITIES

A thousand words is worth a picture

Focus	Vocabulary review
Level	All
Time	5-10 minutes
ICT Skills	Taking pictures with mobile phones; uploading pictures to blogs or wikis (optional)
Preparation	None

in class

1 Get into the habit of keeping the words you write on the board. Instead of erasing them to make room for some more, open new pages as needed.

2 In the closing stages of your lesson, show the pages on the board with the words you wrote and invite the students to take photographs of the board with their mobile phones, thus taking the vocabulary with them. Even if they have already written the words down in their notebooks, this is still a good way for them to double check once they get home. Then they can write them down on paper if they like keeping vocabulary lists, or they can read them aloud and make audio recordings or you can ask them to use the words to write down a few sentences that are true of themselves.

Variation 1

Every week give a different student the responsibility for taking photographs of the words on the board. Hand over a camera (or your phone) to the student in charge in the last few minutes of the lesson. Then upload the photographs to a Powerpoint document or to an IWB companion software every other week or so. Show the photographs in class and review some of the words and expressions with the students. For instance, show one photograph, ask your students to look away for a few seconds and then open your "desktop annotate" tool in Activinspire or "transparent background" in Notebook or "screen annotation" in Mimio (or the equivalent tool from your companion software) and place blotches of ink over sections of words. Ask the students to guess what the words are. Repeat this with a few other photographs. Or show a photograph with annotations and ask the students to work in pairs for a few minutes and test each other on the meaning of the words they see. Or ask pairs of students to construct a short story using at least three or four words or expressions from the board. Elicit answers from the class.

Variation 2

If you have a blog or a wiki for the class, keep a page or section for these annotations and upload the photographs regularly. Then, instead of taking photographs of the board, you can simply access your blog or wiki in class and show the photographs from them.

A thousand words is worth a picture

Variation 3

Instead of using your companion software to annotate vocabulary, use online whiteboards such as Twiddla or TypeWith. Then ask the students to write down the URLs of those whiteboards and access the generated annotations after school. In addition to annotations, these boards also allow users to upload images, Word, Powerpoint and PDF documents. If you have students with Internet connected devices in the classroom, such as laptops or tablets, they can actually interact from their seats with the contents generated on the board and add their own annotations, type text, upload images, etc.

Follow-up

If you have a blog or a wiki, encourage your students to take photographs with their mobile phones or cameras of English words they come across on billboards, in newspapers or magazines, on film posters, graffiti, etc. As in Variation 2, keep a section or page for those photographs. Take a look at them in class from time to time, and highlight interesting vocabulary.

Changes

Focus	Functional language: Describing people; clothes;
	Grammar: Present continuous
Level	Beginner to Pre-intermediate
Time	10–15 minutes
ICT Skills	Copying and pasting images; annotating on the board; grouping

Preparation

1 Find on the Internet a photograph of a party where various people can be seen. These two search queries have prompted good results for this activity: "housewarming party", "dinner party".

2 Copy and paste that photograph onto two blank pages. Enlarge the photograph on the first page so that it takes up the whole page.

in class

1 After teaching or reviewing vocabulary for physical description and/or clothes, display the photograph that you selected for this activity. Ask the students to work in pairs and describe what they can see (e.g. *the woman in the red dress is holding a glass; the man to her right is smiling; he's wearing an orange T-shirt; he has spiky hair,* etc.). Elicit answers from the class.

2 Now invite a student to come up to the front and make a couple of changes to the picture. For instance, by selecting the pen tool and drawing a moustache, extra hair, changing the colour of someone's jacket, making a person smile, frown or cry, making people hold something in their hands, making people disappear, etc.

Picture A
Making changes to a picture

Picture B
Spot the changes

3   Invite three or four more students, one at a time, to the front to make more changes.

4   Now group the picture and the annotations and scale it down to half its size. Go to the second page of your document and copy (or cut) and paste the picture placed there onto the first page. Ask students to work in pairs and compare the pictures (e.g. *In picture A the man wearing an orange shirt is bald but in picture B he has curly brown hair.In picture B the woman in the red dress is gone*, etc.).

In Picture B the superhero has a yellow circle on his shirt now. He has a beard and he is playing the piano. The man on the left is wearing a blue shirt and the man next to him is wearing a red hat. There are some balloons hanging from the ceiling. There are some red roses on the shelf and there aren't any flags now.

Variation 1

Instead of using a group picture, copy and paste single pictures of people showing a variety of ages, builds, clothes and hairstyles. For example you can google the following: "man in an orange shirt"/"girl in flip flops"/"bald man"/"woman with long blonde hair", etc. Then copy and paste each picture twice on a page for the students to make changes to the pictures placed on the left of each page. Ask the students to compare the picture on the left with the picture on the right on each page.

Variation 2

Click on the pen tool and set the colour to white. Then run the pen tool over the picture until it's all covered in white (you may need to adjust the thickness of the pen tool first). Invite a student to come to the front and use the eraser tool to gradually erase sections of that blotch of ink. Ask the students what is being revealed.

Follow-up

Invite about 10 students to the front of the class to pose for a picture and take a picture of them. Ask the participating students to wear different clothes to class next day you teach them. Upload the picture to a page. Show this page and invite these students to stand in front of the class again. Ask the remaining students to say sentences about what they were wearing then and what they are wearing now.

1.3 Chindogu

Focus	Functional language: Describing objects; explaining what things are used for
Level	Intermediate to Upper-intermediate
Time	30–40 minutes
ICT Skills	Copying and pasting images; using a webcam

Preparation

1   Access the Wikipedia article on "chindogu" and also visit these websites where you can find information and images on the subject.

www.chindogu.com http://www.tofugu.com/2012/02/20/chindogu-useless-japanese-inventions/ (http://bit.ly/xaP80S) (shortened link)

http://weburbanist.com/2013/06/26/chindogu-14-hilarious-and-strange-japanese-inventions/ (http://bit.ly/19CwYKI) (shortened link)

Chindogu is the Japanese art of inventing ingenious everyday gadgets that seem like an ideal solution to a particular problem. However, chindogu has a distinctive feature: anyone actually attempting to use one of these inventions would find that it causes so many new problems, or such significant social embarrassment, that it has no utility whatsoever (adapted from Wikipedia).

2   Select about six interesting, and funny–, pictures of these inventions from the suggested sites and copy and paste them on different pages from your IWB companion software or slides from Powerpoint.

in class

1   Give your students a couple of minutes to write down a list of the top five inventions ever. Then elicit answers from the students and ask questions such as: *How has this invention changed people's lives?/ How has this invention changed your life?/ Are there any downsides to it?*

2   Introduce the concept of chindogu to the class. You may access the Wikipedia article and show a picture that you have not included in the document that you saved.

3   Now ask the students to work in pairs. You will show six different pictures of crazy inventions. When you show the first one, Student A should look at the board and try to describe the object and say what it might be used for. Meanwhile Student B, without looking at the board, should draw the object from what she hears on a piece of paper. Give them about two minutes.

4   Students change roles. Repeat this procedure for the remaining pictures.

5   Now collect drawings from various students, open the camera tool on your computer (or use the SMART whiteboard camera)

and place drawings of the first object, one at a time, in front of the camera for the students to see on the board. This will cause hilarity among the students. Go back to your companion software page or Powerpoint slide for the B students to see what the object in question was. Ask the students what they think the purpose of this object is. If you know this yourself, explain. Otherwise, invite the students to do some research later on and explain next time they come to class.

6   Repeat step 5 with the remaining pictures.

Variation 1

You may also try this activity with common objects such as tools (screwdriver, hammer, spanner, wrench, etc.).

Variation 2

If you do variation 1, ask the students to think of alternative uses of those tools, e.g., you may use a screwdriver as a back scratcher, to open a can of paint, to comb your hair, to get mud out of your boots, as a letter opener, etc.

Follow-up

Tell the students to devise a crazy invention and write a description of what it would be used for in about 40–50 words.

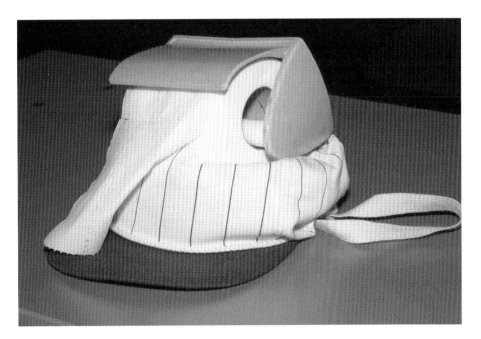

Hay Fever Hat

1.4 Conversation board game

Focus	Speaking: Talking about travelling;
	Writing: Questions
Level	Intermediate
Time	30–45 minutes
ICT Skills	Copying and pasting images
Preparation	1 Find twelve pictures that can illustrate the topic of travel, e.g. a departures lounge at an airport, a taxi, someone packing a suitcase, some travel guide books, a pair of hiking boots, a world map, a beach, a tent, a pedestrian street, a ticket for the underground, a museum and a souvenir shop.
	2 Copy and paste the pictures onto a blank whiteboard page and arrange them as in the picture below, resizing them when necessary. Place a finish square in the middle, thus recreating a board game. Draw some arrows as shown below.

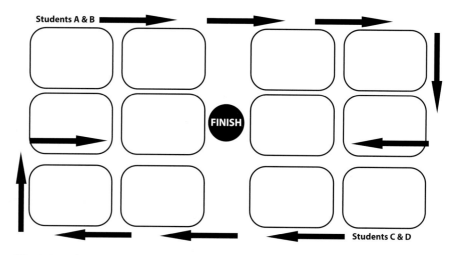

Blank template.
Copy and resize your pictures to fit the squares using your whiteboard software

in class

1 Ask your students to close their eyes for a couple of minutes and imagine they are travelling on a plane. While they have their eyes closed, ask them questions such as *Are you travelling abroad? What are you doing on the plane now? Are you sleeping? Are you eating? Are you watching a film? How far is your final destination? What's the weather like over there? Where are you staying? Are you staying in a nice hotel? Are you sleeping in a tent? What is the first thing you are going to do once you drop off your luggage? Picture yourself wherever you are going to, whether it's a crowded city or perhaps somewhere off the beaten track. What can you see? What can you smell? What can you hear? What are you doing?*

2   After two minutes, ask them to open their eyes again and share their mental images with a partner. Ask two or three students to share with the whole class as well.(e.g.*I was travelling to Cancun and I was already eating Mexican food on the plane. The plane was just a couple of hours away from Mexico City, then I had to catch a connecting flight to Cancun, where I booked a really nice 4 star hotel,* etc.)

3   Now open the document you created and explain that it is a board game for them to have conversations around the theme of travel. Ask the students if they have trouble seeing any of the pictures. If so, enlarge momentarily the view of those pictures, so they can get a brief look in detail.

4   Ask students to work in groups of three or four. One or two students in the group should start the game from the bottom right corner and move anticlockwise and the remaining students should start from the top left corner and move clockwise. Each group needs a coin to toss. Heads move one square and tails move two.

5   Student A tosses the coin. As the groups do not have a copy of the game on their desks, each student must remember where they have landed. Students B, C and D have now about 30 seconds to write a question each related to the picture where Student A has landed. For instance, for the picture of a departures lounge, the students can write questions such as *When was the last time you flew? How often do you fly? How do you spend your time at airports? How many airports have you been to?* Then Student A has to speak for a minute answering one, two or the three questions written by the other students in the group.

6   The students repeat step 5 in turn. When students land on the same square, the groups can decide if they want to use the questions they have already written for that square or write new questions. Early finishers can play another round, this time starting from the opposite end of the board. Walk around the classroom, spot and correct any mistakes when students are writing their questions and provide help for word accuracy and pronunciation.

7   In plenary mode, choose three or four pictures from the board and elicit questions from the students. Invite students to give answers. Answer those questions yourself personally.

Variation 1

   If you have a digital copy of the textbook, take screenshots of interesting pictures from three or four units. Then ask students to create questions based on the topics being illustrated by the pictures and try to incorporate the vocabulary and expressions that they have learned.

Conversation board game

Variation 2

Alternatively you can use online mindmapping tools like Padlet (www.padlet.com), Popplet (www.popplet.com) or Linoit (www. linoit.com). Make sure you number each picture. Share the generated link with the students and ask them to write at least one question per picture on pieces of paper. They should write the question on one side and write the number of the picture they are writing the question for on the other side. Then the students work in groups of three or four in class. They place the questions face down on the table and start the game.

Variation 3

Anticipate about three or four interesting lexical items for each picture and give each group a handout listing those items. Encourage students to use these items in their questions and answers. For example for the picture of a departures lounge you could write *departures lounge, go to gate, delayed flight.*

Variation 4

Find random pictures from the Internet without a common clear thread if you have about ten spare minutes at the end of the lesson for some general speaking practice.

Follow-up

Based on one of the three or four images that you drew attention to in plenary mode, ask students to write a blog entry (digitally, if you have a class blog, or on paper) of 50–100 words. If you wrote useful vocabulary or expressions on the board, encourage students to incorporate some. Then next day you can ask a few students to read out their texts or, if they posted them on a blog, show the selected texts on the whiteboard and highlight good use of vocabulary or ask the class to correct any mistakes.

Every bedroom tells a story

Focus	Vocabulary for things in the house; bedrooms; Talking about likes and dislikes
Level	Beginner to Elementary
Time	20–25 minutes
ICT Skills	Taking pictures, copying and pasting images

Preparation

1   Ask volunteer students to shoot some digital pictures of their bedrooms and either email them to you or save them in pen drives. Each student may take two or three pictures from different angles so that they can show the rooms in more detail.

2   Retrieve the pictures from the emails or the pen drives, scale them down and place them at the bottom of a blank page, leaving some distance in between pictures sent by the different participating students.

in class

1   Ask the students to brainstorm words for things that are typically found in a bedroom. Elicit answers and ask a student write the words on the board.

2   Open the document. Drag one picture to the middle of the screen and enlarge it. Ask the students to tell you what they can see in the picture. Write key vocabulary on the board. Scale this picture down and drag it to the bottom of the screen. Erase the annotations. Drag another picture to the middle and follow the same procedure.

3   Now bring a different picture (or a set of different pictures if the student has taken different pictures of the same room) and give the students some time to think about what kinds of things he/ she may enjoy doing based on what they can see on the board. For instance if they can see a lot of videogames or books or a guitar or a poster, they may say: *Joana likes reading Harry Potter novels, she enjoys playing World of Warcraft, she can play the guitar, she loves Jimi Hendrix,* etc. Repeat the procedure with the remaining pictures from the bottom of the screen.

4   Now, based on the generated sentences, ask the students to think of follow-up questions for the pictures. At the suggested language level these are possible expected questions: *What's your favourite Harry Potter book and why? Are you reading a novel at the moment? What can you play on the guitar? Do you take music lessons? Where? Can you play other musical instruments? Do you have a game console? What games do you have?* The students who sent these pictures give their answers to the class.

Every bedroom tells a story

5   Ask the students to imagine they are holding a paper photograph of their bedroom. In pairs or small groups the students share these imaginary images and describe and talk about their bedrooms and the things they keep in them. Encourage the class to ask follow-up questions as they did with the real digital photographs taken by some of the students.

Variation 1

This activity can also be done with pictures from the Internet (in this case you would skip step 3), which might be more suitable if you feel you have a substantial number of students in your class who would not be comfortable showing their own bedrooms. However, the activity is much more effective when personal pictures are brought to class.

Variation 2

Instead of taking pictures of bedrooms, the students may take pictures of objects that are meaningful to them or that they relate to, e.g. one student may bring to class a picture of a book, a guitar, a videogame and a goldfish.

Variation 3

Instead of bedrooms the students may bring photographs of their living-rooms.

Follow-up

Ask the students to take a photograph of their bedroom, copy and paste it onto a text editing program and write a text of 50–70 words about it. Invite them to print a copy. Decorate the classroom with the resulting documents.

1.6

Five things

Focus Speaking: Making personal presentations

Level Pre-intermediate to Intermediate

Time 20 minutes for Day 1; 10 minutes for Day 2

ICT Skills Copying and pasting images; using Powerpoint or online visual presentation tools

Preparation Choose five personal photographs and create a personal presentation with Powerpoint, your IWB companion software or a visual presentation online tool such as Voicethread or Prezi. Paste each picture onto a different slide or page. You can show photographs that reflect your hobbies, such as playing a sport, gardening or walking your dog. Ideally, you should be choosing photographs that may reveal things about you that your students do not know about (yet). This activity works best at the onset of the school year.

in class

Day 1

1   Open your document and tell the students that you are going to make a short personal presentation illustrated by a few personal pictures. You will be sharing with them five things they may not know about you. Stay on each slide or page for about a minute or two and elaborate on what's conveyed by the pictures. For lower levels you may want to give your students some lexical input prior to your presentation (e.g. *in this picture you can see... / in the foreground... in the background...* prepositions of place, etc.).

2   Now ask the students if they have any questions for you.

3   Ask students to work in groups of four or five. Each student must choose a personal photograph and tell the group about it. These photographs may be real or imaginary. Real photographs may be shown from their smartphones. If they do not have smartphones or they'd rather not show them, they may share imaginary pictures. In that case, they can show the palms of their hands and pretend they are holding a photograph. (you may want to model this first).They would then describe the photograph. You can write these questions on the board to help them with their presentations:
    - why is this picture important to you?
    - when was it taken?
    - where was it taken?
    - who took it?
    - what can you see?

4   In plenary mode, ask a few students to share their (real or imaginary) pictures with everyone else.

5   Tell the students to prepare a short personal presentation using visual aids, as you just did at the beginning of the lesson. This presentation must include five pictures.

It is not imperative that they appear in the pictures. They can choose a picture of a place they like or they know well, or show a picture of a guitar if they enjoy playing that instrument, or a picture of a pet. The presentation should last approximately five to seven minutes. Ask for a volunteer to agree to do the next presentation on Day 2.

Day 2

1 Start off the lesson with a personal presentation from a student.
2 Invite the students to ask questions.
3 Ask for a different student to promise to start off the following lesson with a personal presentation.

Variation 1

Show each picture for about 30 seconds. Do not say anything about them. Invite your students to think of questions for the pictures they are seeing. Then let the students ask you questions and answer them.

Variation 2

Include one "lie" in your presentation. Then reveal that four of the things you talked about are true and one is not. Challenge the class to guess what the lie was.

Variation 3

Type about 10 statements related to your presentation and print copies for the students. Alternatively read out these statements in class prior to the presentation and ask the students to write them down. You could include five items that are true and five that are not. Ask the class to check the ones that they think are true. Elicit a few answers. Then give your presentation for the students to confirm or rectify their guesses.

Follow-up

Introduce Voicethread to your class and invite volunteer students to create presentations online and make them available to everyone. Then encourage them to record and place questions on those presentations for the creators to answer.

A personal photograph

1.7 From Italy to Brazil and back again

Focus	Writing and speaking: About their own countries
Level	Pre-intermediate to Upper-intermediate
Time	20–30 minutes for Day 1; 15–25 minutes for Day 2
ICT Skills	Creating a presentation on Voicethread
Preparation	1 Get in touch with an international class of students who are studying English. The further resources section in this book offers useful information on finding other classes internationally. Preview with their teacher the visual presentation tool Voicethread and get familiar with how to use it.

   2   Create an account for your class (and have the partner teacher create another account for her class) and plan a project where both classes will have to create a visual presentation reflecting various aspects of life in their own countries. Agree on a some topics or categories for the presentations, e.g. choose a few among these: food, traditions, sports, places to visit, art, curious facts, famous people, lifestyle, things that hardly anyone knows or history. Ideally both classes would have a similar level of language competency but this is not essential.

   3   Set up deadlines for the students to create the content and share their presentations online.

in class

Day 1

1   Write the name of the country where the partner class is and ask the students what they know about it. Has anyone been there? What do they know about its food, traditions, sports, etc.? If the students have Internet connected devices in the classroom, give them two or three minutes to find out interesting facts about this country for them to share afterwards. These are useful links:

- www.lonelyplanet.com (they should type "Germany" or any other country in the search box)

- www.havetravelfun.com (again, type "Germany" in the search box)

- www.europa.eu (thorough and creditable for EU countries)

2   Open Voicethread on your Web browser and show the students its main features. Users can create visual presentations by uploading pictures and they can also type text, add annotations and incorporate voice and video recordings. In addition, if the link of any given presentation is shared, other users can also interact with it by typing or/and recording their own comments. Try out the tool in front of the students for them to see. Provide links with tutorials for them to get familiar with the tool.

3   Explain that you have devised a joint project with a school in the country they have just been talking about. Explain the aim of the

project on Voicethread. You will be setting up six groups. You have started a presentation for them containing six blank slides. Each group's task will be to fill up their slide with an image illustrating their chosen category. In addition, each group member must place an audio recording containing relevant information on the assigned topic. Give the students the link and password for the Voicethread account so that they can edit the content of this presentation. Establish a deadline for the students to complete their work.

4   Exchange links for the presentations with the partner class by email or via a backchannelling site such as TodaysMeet.

Day 2

1   Review with your class, in plenary mode, your partner class presentation. Listen to a few audio recordings placed on the slides and check understanding.

2   Invite the students to watch the presentation outside school hours and to leave either text or voice comments.

Variation 1

Tell the students to watch the partner class presentation at home. You will then create a quiz with questions based on the information furnished in the presentation. Set up groups and have a quiz show with questions and answers.

Variation 2

As an alternative to a joint project, devise Voicethread presentations for your class about different English-speaking countries. Ask students to work in groups and create a presentation around various aspects of the chosen country through images, text and voice recordings. You may give your students the sites listed above.

Variation 3

Prior to a field trip, such as a visit to a museum, for instance, let the students get familiar with this presentation tool and invite them to create a Voicethread afterwards with pictures taken during this field trip together with their reflections and comments. They may also include recorded interviews with tour guides or curators.

Follow-up

Voicethread could be a very adequate platform for the students to create digital portfolios where they can incorporate samples of work and reflect on the learning process. They may scan handwritten documents, upload images, PDF or Word documents and leave voice recordings. Teachers may also give feedback by means of text or voice comments.

Games children play

Focus	Grammar: Present continuous;
	Speaking: Talking about children's games
Level	Intermediate to Upper-intermediate
Time	20–30 minutes
ICT Skills	Browsing the Web; copying and pasting images; using the spotlight tool (optional)
Preparation	1 Find online the painting *Children's Games* by Pieter Bruegel the Elder (see step 2). This painting from 1560 features over 200 children engaged in 80 different games and activities, from hoop rolling to playing hide and seek. Copy and paste the image onto a blank page and enlarge it so that it fills up the entire space.
	2 Visit the Wikipedia entry for this painting (http://en.wikipedia.org/wiki/Children's_Games_(Bruegel) or shortened link http://bit.ly/Ibqs48). Here you can find an image of the painting and close-ups and explanations of the eighty games that have been identified.

in class

1 Write on the board:

- tag
- hide-and-seek
- marbles

2 Ask the class if they know what these words refer to. Do they know these games? Have they ever played them? How are they played? How old were they the last time they played any of those games? (in order to clarify meaning you may want to find images on the Internet for the students to see). What other traditional games are popular amongst children in their country?

3 Show the painting on the screen now. Can they find children playing tag, hide-and-seek and marbles there?

4 Ask the students to work in pairs or small groups and talk about the painting and try to identify the many games and activities the children are engaged in.

5 Invite the students to come up to the board and point at the games they can see and explain what the children are doing. Help them with vocabulary.

6 Open the spotlight tool and move it around the page to allow certain areas to be seen. Ask the students to describe what's being revealed. Otherwise look for the painting on your Web browser and enlarge the view of the webpage by choosing the zoom in option from the menu. Then use the side and bottom bars of the Web browser to direct attention to different portions of the screen.

7 To wrap things up, ask the class about their favourite toys and

games, whether they were digital or physical, when they were about five to eight years old. Also, tell the students to ask their parents about the games they used to play when they were children and report to the class next day.

Variation 1

A good way to lead in to conversation around a theme is to use a painting that somehow bears a relation to it. Ask the students to look at the painting and unlock the symbols and the story it may be telling. These are some common themes and famous paintings that could be used hand in hand.

- Marriage: *The Arnolfini Portrait* by Jan Van Eyck
- Wealth/Money/Power: *The Ambassadors* by Hans Holbein the Younger
- Death/War/Violence: *Guernica* by Pablo Picasso
- Free time: *A Sunday on La Grande Jatte* by Seurat
- Love/Relationships: *The Kiss* by Gustav Klimt
- Social Justice/Poverty: *The Potato Eaters* by Van Gogh

Variation 2

Ask the students to do some research on this painting and/or Pieter Bruegel the Elder before you do this activity. Start off the lesson asking the students what they found out and then project *Children's Games*.

Children's Games by Pieter Bruegel

Follow-up

Give a list of interesting paintings that can prompt discussion in the classroom at the onset of the school year. Then set up groups in the classroom and have them choose one painting from the list and do research on it. Each week (or month) a group will be in charge of giving a ten minute presentation about this painting. These are some of the aspects they could refer to in their presentation: any possible symbolisms in the painting, the formal qualities, the subject matter, an insight into the artist's life, the historical context, their interpretation, their emotional response, etc.

Guess what just happened

Focus	Grammar: Connectors and sequencers
Level	Elementary to Intermediate
Time	15–20 minutes
ICT Skills	Copying and pasting images
Preparation	Find six to eight pictures of different locations, for instance, a picture of the countryside, an office, a crowded street, a café, a school, a shopping center, and a living room. Copy and paste those pictures onto a slide of your presentation software or online tool.

in class

1   Open the document and ask the class if they can recall when the last time was that they were at a café, shopping centre, etc. What were they doing? Did anything unexpected happen to them?

2   Now write on the board:

I was… when…

Then…

But…

So…

3   Tell the students that you are going to talk about the last time you went to a shopping centre. You will be using the words from the board in your account. Ask them to make a conscious effort to identify them. You may use the example below or your own.

I was at the shopping centre when I saw a pair of football boots that I really liked. Then I walked in the shop to try them on. But they didn't have my size. So I left the shop and walked towards the escalators.

4   Now ask them to choose one of the places from the pictures and write an anecdote in about three to six lines using the connectors and sequencers from the board, as you have just modelled. This short story could be true or they can simply make it up. Circulate to provide help and to make any necessary corrections.

5   The students read out their anecdotes. Encourage the students to ask follow-up questions based on what they have heard.

(The idea for this activity comes from *For Real Elementary*, Martyn Hobbs and Julia Starr Keddle, Helbling Languages, page 100).

Variation 1

Instead of choosing general pictures of places, look for landmarks in your town (the bus station, the main shopping street, a popular fast food restaurant, the school, etc.).

Guess what just happened

Variation 2

For lower levels of English, write *I was, But* and *So.* Ask the students to write their anecdotes in two or three lines using these target words.

For higher levels of English write some of these connecting words: *besides, not only, what's more, as soon as, while, afterwards, meanwhile, however, whereas, even though, despite.*

Follow-up

Ask the students to build on what they have just written in class and expand and polish their stories at home by rewriting them again in a paragraph of about six to ten lines. Encourage use of dictionaries and use of vocabulary that you may have written on the board for them for higher lexical accuracy.

Life's common objects

Focus Vocabulary for common objects

Level Beginner to Pre-intermediate

Time 15–20 minutes

ICT Skills Copying and pasting images; pen tool

Preparation

1 Look for pictures of common objects. For example, if the students are learning words for objects in the classroom, run a search online for pictures of a pencil sharpener, a stapler, a ruler, etc. If they are learning words for things in the house, look for pictures of a bedside table, a lamp, curtains, etc. If they are learning about personal everyday objects then look for pictures of a wallet, a comb, a pair of glasses, a credit card, etc. Other typical lexical sets for the suggested language levels can be food or clothes. A total of ten pictures is a good number.

2 Copy and paste each picture on a different page. Enlarge them so that they take up most of the screen. Now go back to the first picture on the first page and select the pen tool. Draw the outline of the object. Then select the picture, drag it away, scale it down as much as possible so that it becomes impossible to tell what it is and place it in a corner on the page. Repeat this procedure for the remaining pictures.

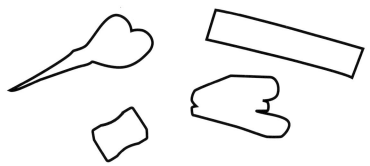

Outlines for pair of scissors, ruler, pencil sharpener and stapler

1 Tell the students that they are going to learn or practise (or review) words for objects in the classroom, things in the house, etc. Have them brainstorm for words they already know. You may also do activities related to this from the textbook, workbook, a handout, the Internet, etc.

2 Now show the document that you created. On every page they will see the outline of an object and a tiny icon in a corner. In some cases the object in question will be more obvious than in others. It is their task to make guesses and see if they can work out what the object is. Only in a very few cases will it be evident what the object is. However, the fact that it can only be something from a very limited range of options will make the students think hard about the target words, thus consolidating the vocabulary in their brains.

3   Ask the students to work in pairs or groups of three or four first. Show the first page for about 15–20 seconds, then move to the second page and wait about the same length of time and so on.

4   When you have shown all the drawings, go back to the first page and now, in plenary mode, elicit answers. Select the picture placed in the corner, enlarge it and drag it to the middle of the screen. Adjust the size so that the outline of the object in the picture and your drawing match. Repeat this for the remaining drawings and pictures.

Variation 1

Place all the objects and drawings on one page. Then scale the drawings down (you may need to group each drawing to make sure that each single drawing moves as a whole and can be enlarged and scaled down). Place the drawings on the top and the pictures on the bottom and drag drawings and pictures as needed to the middle of the screen while enlarging the size.

Variation 2

Ask volunteer students to take a photograph of their face and save it in a pen drive. In class, open the files and copy and paste the photographs on different pages. Set the background colour of the page to white (this is typically the default colour) and choose black as the colour for the pen tool. Ask the students to trace their faces from the photographs and then print copies of those pages with the drawings. The students can then write about themselves and incorporate the printed drawings. Decorate the classroom with the drawings and the samples of writing.

Follow-up

Ask the students to find common objects (no larger than an A4 size piece of paper) e.g. a coin, a bank note, a wallet, a ring, etc. and trace them on paper. Then they bring the papers to class and put them up on the classroom walls. Each piece of paper with a drawing on it is numbered. Each student then gets a pen and a blank piece of paper, stands up, circulates, looks at the numbered drawings and writes down on their paper what they think has been outlined on the numbered papers.

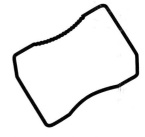

Copy and paste a picture   Trace it with the pen tool   Drag away the picture and leave your drawing.

Myths and facts

Focus	Grammar: Past simple
Level	Elementary to Intermediate
Time	10–15 minutes for Day 1; 15–20 minutes for Day 2
ICT Skills	Using online mindmapping tools
Preparation	None

in class

Day 1

1   Open the online mapping tool Padlet and show your students how to use it. Better still, you can ask a student a few days before you are planning to do this activity to have a look at this online tool at home and then show the class. Other alternative tools for this activity are www.linoit.com or www.popplet.com.

2   Create a document on your chosen mapping tool and share the generated URL with the class. Tell the students to copy down the URL. You may want to shorten the URL using a URL shrinker like bitly.com. Padlet has also the option to generate your own links (e.g. www.padlet.com/wall/mrbrownenglishclass).

3   Let the students choose two or three well-known people in the field of sports or music. Then ask them to do some research on these people outside school hours. Wikipedia is a good enough source of information for this activity. They should read about the people and take notes and then go to the unique URL for the mapping tool and type sentences about them using the past simple. The sentences may be true or not e.g, they can type *Neymar played for Santos in Brazil* (which is true) or *Neymar joined Barcelona FC in 2012* (which is not true).

Day 2

1   Open the URL for the mapping tool in class and ask a student to read out a typed statement from the whiteboard. Is it true or not? If not, invite them to correct it (e.g. *Neymar joined Barcelona in 2012 No, he didn't. He joined the team in 2013*). They should also edit the text on the computer to make the statement true. Repeat the procedure for all the typed statements.

2   Finally tell the students to go online and access the Wikipedia entries for the selected people and check whether all the corrections made in class were accurate or not.

Variation 1

As an extension to the activity, create a quiz game with questions based on the generated statements. You may simply write down your questions on paper and read them out to the students or do this digitally by creating an interactive quiz show from www.polleverywhere.com.

 **Myths and facts**

Variation 2

This activity focuses on practical use of the past simple but you may choose present simple as the target structure. Another interesting approach would be to contrast past simple and present perfect.

Follow-up

Ask the students to write a biography of a family member or a friend. They may write this biography on paper, they may use a computer and email it to you or they can use an online presentation tool such as Prezi, Narrable or Voicethread, and combine text with images.

1.12 Our world

Focus	Talking and writing about meaningful objects
Level	All
Time	5-10 minutes for Day 1; 20-30 minutes for Day 2
ICT Skills	Using online mindmapping tools
Preparation	None

in class

Day 1

1 As in Activity 1.11, introduce your students to online mapping tools like Padlet, Linoit or Popplet (or ask a student beforehand to take at look at these tools and then show the class for you).

2 Create a document with the mapping tool of your choice and share the generated URL with the class. Tell the students to copy down the URL. Tell the students to, outside school hours, place on it a picture of something they identify with and which is meaningful to them. It could either be a personal picture or a picture from the Internet. As examples, suggest pictures of an electric guitar, a mobile phone, a laptop, their room, a film they like, an album cover, a book cover, or a pet to name a few. Explain that the next day you will be opening the document in class for them to have conversations around these pictures.

Day 2

1 Open the document and ask the students to work in pairs or groups of three and discuss which pictures they think have been placed by their classmates.

2 Elicit a few answers and then let the students who placed those pictures tell the class about them.

3 Get the students into groups of five or six to talk about the pictures that they placed on this document. If there are students who did not post a picture on the mapping tool, make sure that they are evenly placed in the groups so that each group is made up of students who can talk about the pictures that they posted and students who can ask questions.

4 Now in plenary mode invite the students to talk about why those pictures (or what they represent) are important to them (e.g. *I picked this picture because...; I'm really fond of this picture because...; I'm keen on...; This picture means a lot to me as...*).

Variation 1

In addition to placing images, ask the students to write a couple of sentences about them on the mindmapping tool as well. They should keep the sentences short and simple so as not to overload the screen with text.

Variation 2

Based on the images that they see, ask the students to think of questions they could ask to get them talking about the objects on the screen. Then elicit those questions.

Variation 3

Ask the students to find an image of the cover of a book that they have read and enjoyed. You could pre-teach some useful words and expressions and invite them to place the image on the mapping tool and also write about 20–40 words using those words. At an Advanced level you could ask them to use phrases and expressions such as *the plot centres on…/a page-turner/I couldn't put the book down/a very timely book/a gripping story/a must-read.*

At an Intermediate to Advanced level other possible themes are films (in which case the students can either place images or embed video trailers), inventions or historical events. At an Elementary to Pre-intermediate level you may adapt this activity for physical descriptions or clothes.

Follow-up

Ask the students to write about what's meaningful to them in more depth and post this to a blog or a wiki.

Personal pictures

Focus	Speaking: Talking about personal pictures;
	Grammar: Frequency adverbs
Level	Pre-intermediate to Intermediate
Time	25–35 minutes
ICT Skills	Using a webcam
Preparation	None

in class

1 Ask the students if they know what a pie chart is (a chart the shape of a circle divided into sectors which looks like a sliced pie and shows numerical proportions). Type "pie chart" on Google and click on images for them to see. Ask them *Where can one find pie charts and what are they used for?*

2 Now ask students to get a piece of paper, draw a big circle on it and create a pie chart showing how they use their phone. You may draw one example on the board like this one:

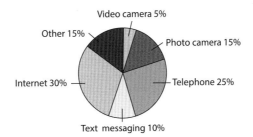

Use of smartphone

They may use the words from your pie chart or their own, depending on their most frequent use of the phone. Explain that the chart obviously shows an estimate.

3 Ask the students to stand up, mill around, compare their pie charts and talk about them. Write on the board a list of frequency adverbs (*always, usually, often, sometimes, hardly ever, never*) for the students to try to elaborate sentences using them (e.g. *I hardly ever send text messages these days; I always use What'sApp to send text messages; I sometimes record videos and upload them to Facebook*, etc).

4 Tell the students to go back to their seats and ask them about the use of the smartphone as a photo camera. e.g. *What number did you write for use of phone as a photo camera?* for the students to call out their numbers.

5 Ask the students to work into groups of three to five. They should select one photo from their phone that they feel comfortable showing and, in turns, talk about it for about a minute. They can definitely

describe what can be seen in the photograph but they may also explain what they were doing at the time, why they decided to take it, etc.

Give the students enough time to find the pictures and ask them not to show them until they have located them (sometimes additional pictures which the students might not be comfortable with may be revealed in album views). If there are students within a group that do not have a phone or pictures on it or they do not want to show them and talk about them, it is still fine to have a group of about four to six students where you have three or four students sharing their pictures.

6 Now ask for one volunteer to come up to the front with his/her phone. Open the camera tool of the computer and ask this student to place the phone in front of the camera lens for the photograph to be displayed on the board so that everyone can see. Invite this student to describe this picture.

7 Finally write this on the board: - *Do you think...?*

Ask the class to think of questions using the prompt given that could be relevant for the photograph they have just seen. For example, if it was a picture taken at a birthday party, these might be interesting questions to ask:- *Do you think you will invite the same friends for your next birthday? Do you think they were generous with the presents? Do you think you will be celebrating your birthday there again? Do you think your friends had a good time?*

Variation 1

Ask the students to take a few pictures with their phones over the weekend of things they will be doing. Then on Monday (or the first day of the week you see them) start off your lesson with the students sharing those pictures and talking about them.

Variation 2

In connection with a topic that you are currently discussing in class, ask the students to find any photos on their phones that might bear an association with it. This might be easier with some topics than others. It works really well with family, friends, hobbies, free time, school, jobs, the environment, home or technology, for instance.

Variation 3

Ask your students to take photos of their typical day at school.

Follow-up

Set up a schedule for the students to, in turns, share a personal photograph with the classroom (once a week or every other week) by means of their mobile phone and the camera tool in the computer. Alternatively, they can select a photograph from their mobile phone and copy and paste it onto a slide in a presentation tool of their choice (e.g. Powerpoint/ Keynote/ Voicethread/ Prezi/ Emaze).

Personalizing the textbook

Focus	Speaking: Talking about pictures
Level	All
Time	25–30 minutes
ICT Skills	Copying and pasting images
Preparation	Select a textbook page that includes at least one picture that is used to illustrate a topic. In many instances, a few conversation questions around the topic go hand in hand with the picture. If you have a digital version of the textbook, show the page on your board. Otherwise, ask the students to open their books on that page.

in class

1   Open the document showing the textbook page. Focus the class attention on the picture/s and elicit answers from the students regarding the question/s provided by the textbook. Write useful words and expressions on the sides.

2   Now ask the students to work in pairs or groups of three, and think of one additional question that could be relevant to the picture and the topic it illustrates. Invite the students to share their questions and answers.

3   Ask the pairs or groups to provide a search query phrase that will be used to look for alternative images for the textbook page. In this case I will use as an example an article on "20 things to do before you die" *from For Real Elementary*, Martyn Hobbs and Julia Starr Keddle, Helbling Languages. The article is illustrated by six pictures showing a Formula One car, a couple dancing tango, a young man sailing, etc. There is an accompanying speaking task asking the students to work in groups and think of four more things to do before dying. Then the students, in their groups, may suggest search queries for Google images such as "riding a motorbike"/"bungee jumping"/"planting a tree"/"writing a book"/"newborn baby", etc.

4   Look for those images by typing the search queries on Google and ask the class to agree to choose five to seven relevant pictures. Copy and paste those pictures onto a blank page. Now ask the students to think of interesting conversation questions regarding those pictures. For instance, around the picture of a motorbike, the students could generate e.g. *Who has a motorbike? How often do you ride it? Is it dangerous to ride a motorbike? In which ways is a motorbike better than a car? What's more exciting: riding a motorbike or going bungee jumping?* Let the students discuss these questions.

Personalizing the textbook

Variation 1

If you have a digital copy of the textbook you can use screen capture tools, such as the Snipping Tool from Windows (start >all programmes > accessories > snipping tool), and take a snapshot of the textbook page. Place the resulting image on a blank page and then place the selected image/s from the image search on top of the picture/s included in the textbook page (you may need to scale down the images and/or change their layering to top layer).

Note: for further instructions on how to use the Snipping Tool, access this link from the Microsoft site: http://windows.microsoft.com/en-us/windows-vista/use-snipping-tool-to-capture-screen-shots or run this search on Google: "how to use the snipping tool in Windows".

Variation 2

Ask students to do step 3 individually at home. Then each student can print out a couple of pictures for discussion in class next time. Alternatively, they can store their pictures in their mobile phones or tablets and show them from those devices.

Follow-up

Based on the idea from variation 1, instead of replacing the pictures, ask the students to think of alternative texts to replace the text/s found on the selected page. In the example used, there is a short reading passage on things to do before dying. The students could type those texts at home and then email them to you. Take a snapshot of a sample of writing and next place it over the reading passage; thus replacing it (again you may need to scale it down and make sure that it goes to the top layer) with the student's text.

1.15 Proverbs

Focus	Discussing English proverbs
Level	Intermediate to Advanced
Time	30–40 minutes
ICT Skills	Browsing the Web; copying and pasting images; typing text

Preparation

1 Find on the Internet the painting *Netherlandish Proverbs* by Pieter Bruegel the Elder. In this painting from 1559 we can find a depiction of over 100 proverbs or parables. Some of these proverbs have modern English equivalents. These are useful shortened links:

- http://en.wikipedia.org/wiki/Netherlandish_Proverbs (short link: http://bit.ly/3Gxjjw): Wikipedia article featuring information on the painting as well as a list of the identified proverbs, their meanings and detailed views of the depicted proverbs.

- http://s3.imagediver.org/topic/album/4294b0e/the_dutch_proverbs/1/index.html (short link: http://bit.ly/15afbp3): Displays a copy of the painting with framed areas for the various identified proverbs. It includes a zoom-in tool. Ideal for interactive whiteboards.

- http://smarthistory.khanacademy.org/bruegel-the-dutch-proverbs.html (short link: http://bit.ly/143HG7F): A short video from Khan Academy with commentaries from Dr. Beth Harris and Dr. Steven Zucker.

2 Find four interesting proverbs depicted in the painting; take snapshots of the corresponding areas and place them on a slide in a presentation tool of your choice (e.g. Powerpoint/ Keynote/ Voicethread/ Prezi/ Emaze) or a page from your companion software. Otherwise, copy and paste them from the first link provided. Find the proverbs and meanings on the Wikipedia article. Type the chosen proverbs on the bottom left corner of the screen in any order. Type the meanings of the proverbs on the bottom right corner of the screen in any order. Create and place solid objects over the typed proverbs and meanings to hide the view.

3 Finally select about fifteen different proverbs from the painting and write them down on a piece of paper.

in class

1 Tell the class that you are going to have conversations around proverbs. Give them about five minutes to think about English proverbs that they know or they remember.

2 Elicit proverbs from the students. What do those proverbs mean? Do they agree? Can they find real life situations where those proverbs could be applied? Do those proverbs have an equivalent in their L1?

3 Now tell your class about the painting *Netherlandish Proverbs*. You may access the Wikipedia article for them to have a quick look at the painting and a quick read at the article. Alternatively you may provide them with handouts with some information on the matter. What's their impression of the painting? Had they seen it before?

4 Now open the document that you created. Tell the students that they can see four details of the painting featuring four proverbs. In pairs or threes, they should think of at least one proverb for one of the paintings. This could be an existing proverb that they know in English or a made up one. Reassure them that, although hard as this may seem, you are ultimately interested in their creativity.

5 Elicit possible proverbs from the students and ask them what the connection is between the selected images on the board and their proverbs.

6 Now reveal the proverbs on the bottom left corner. Can they match them with the images? What do those proverbs mean?

7 Reveal the meanings on the bottom right corner. Ask the students to match proverbs and meanings. Can they find real life situations where those proverbs could be applied?

8 Finally explore the painting with your class. Read out, one at time, the selected proverbs and see if the students can spot where they can be found in the painting.

It is ill to swim against the stream

The die is cast

To throw one's money into the water

Two fools under one hood

1.15 Proverbs

Variation 1

An interesting way to lead in to the activity would be to create a word poster with about ten proverbs on Wordle and display it in class for the students to try to find them.

How many proverbs can you get?

Variation 2

If you try variation 1 as a lead-in, ask the students to create Wordle posters with about six to eight proverbs. Tell them to print copies and bring them to class. Then the students can work in groups, have a look at the copies and try to guess what the hidden proverbs are.

Variation 3

Use inverted commas to run a search for about ten well-known English proverbs on Google Images. Select one image for each of the proverbs. Paste the pictures onto a page. Can they guess the proverbs? Give them hints when they are having trouble guessing.

Follow-up

Encourage the students to explore the painting outside school hours. Also, ask them to do some research on English proverbs. Can they find…

a …one proverb that translates literally into their L1?

b …one proverb that relates to the same concept but does not translate literally into their L1?

c …one proverb whose wording and concept cannot be found in their L1? (this is particularly interesting, as the concept will probably be challenged by some students).

Ask them to discuss their findings in class next day.

1.16 Ranking

Focus	Vocabulary for fruit
Level	Beginner to Elementary
Time	10–20 minutes
ICT Skills	Copying and pasting images
Preparation	Find about 10–14 images of fruits and copy and paste them onto a blank page. Scale them down and place them on the bottom half of the screen.

in class

1 Show the document that you have created with the pictures of fruits. Introduce, or review, the vocabulary with the students and drill pronunciation.

2 Ask the students to get some paper and write down a list of the top five fruits that they would take on a school trip from the ones that they can see on the board. Give them about a minute and then ask for a volunteer to come to the front and drag five pictures to the top of the screen. Ask a few other students which words they wrote down.

3 Drag the five pictures down to the bottom of the screen. Repeat step 2 but change the criterion each time. These are other possible criteria: top five fruits in terms of roundness; five most expensive fruits; five cheapest fruits; five biggest fruits; five smallest fruits; five heaviest fruits; five sweetest fruits; five fruits that grow in your region; five most exotic fruits; the most difficult to spell; the most difficult to pronounce; the most difficult to learn; five fruits you like the best.

(This activity is an adaptation from Andrew Wright's *The Best Fruit, Pictures for Language Learning*, CUP, 1989.)

Variation 1

Tell the students to close their eyes (or not to look at the board) for a few seconds. Then delete (or cut) four or five pictures. Tell them to look at the board. Which pictures are missing?

Variation 2

Arrange the pictures in a row (or two rows depending on the number) and ask the students to look at them for about 30 seconds. Then open a new blank page. Can they recall the order? Go back to the first page and rearrange the pictures in a different order for them to try a second time.

Variation 3

You may also focus on many other lexical areas for the suggested language level , e.g. jobs, sports, clothes, furniture, school subjects, free time activities or places in town. Teenagers may enjoy taking a look at music genres, junk food, mobile devices, social networking sites, things to spend money on, videogames.

Variation 4

In addition to providing vocabulary consolidation, this teaching technique can also be a springboard for conversation around certain themes. For instance, at an Intermediate to Advanced level, find pictures of a tent, a caravan, a bed and breakfast, a five-star hotel, a group of people hiking, a beach, mountains, a cruise ship, a swimming pool, a country house, a summer language school. Then provide the following criteria for the students to rank them: your favourite type of holiday; the most relaxing; the most tiring; the most expensive; types of holidays you have never tried; the ones with lesser ecological impact; the most popular in your country/region; the most romantic

Then think of interesting questions to ask the class, e.g. *Why do you think staying in a caravan is more romantic than staying at a bed and breakfast? So you went camping last summer, how did it go? Did you have a good time? Was there anything that you didn't like about sleeping in a tent?*

Variation 5

For more advanced levels and focusing again on conversation rather than on vocabulary consolidation, simply type the words on a page instead of placing pictures. For instance, you can ask the students to rank the five most essential qualities of a teacher or a friend or a politician and then elaborate on their choices.

Follow-up

For homework, tell the students to think of one or two other criteria that were not discussed in class and rank the words. Then, in class, they read out their rankings without saying what the criteria are for the rest of the students to guess what the criteria in question are.

1.17 Say it with a painting

Focus	Vocabulary review
Level	All
Time	5–10 minutes
ICT Skills	Copying and pasting images
Preparation	Find some images of intriguing paintings. This activity works well with *Triple Elvis* by Andy Warhol, *The Kiss* by Gustav Klimt, *Composition VII* by Kandinsky, *Red Balloon* by Paul Klee and *Nighthawks* by Edward Hopper. Copy and paste the images onto a slide of your presentation tool of your choice (e.g. Powerpoint/ Keynote/ Voicethread/ Prezi/ Emaze) or a page from your companion software.

in class

1   In the last ten minutes of a lesson ask your students to take a look at the vocabulary that they have written in their notebooks or underlined in the textbooks or handouts.

2   Now open the document that you created. Give them two or three minutes to form associations and to use some of those words and phrases as part of alternative titles for the paintings. Give them an example, e.g. if you wrote on the board *hum a song* about half an hour ago, say *OK, my alternative title for "Nighthawks" is "Hum a song, Sam" because we can see a bar and this kind of reminds me of "Casablanca" and the scene with the line "Play it, Sam".*

3   Elicit alternative titles for the paintings from the students and invite them to explain why they made each particular association.

Variation 1

Use interesting photographs, music album covers or film posters instead of paintings.

Variation 2

Recycle the paintings after you have tried this activity a few times.

Follow-up

Have a discussion with your students on how to record vocabulary next time you see them after you have tried this activity. What do they do to learn and remember vocabulary? Do they keep vocabulary lists? How many different ways can they think of to record vocabulary? How can technology be applied to help them record and review it? Explain that forming associations between the paintings and the words and expressions, as in the activity above, is an effective way of consolidating vocabulary, as we retrieve information better when we create mental images or we create links or connections. Also, playing around with those words in our minds involves a considerable degree of cognitive depth, which helps out committing those new words to long-term memory.

1.18

Speak, spoke, spoken

Focus	Grammar: Past simple and past participle of irregular verbs
Level	Beginner to Intermediate
Time	10–20 minutes
ICT Skills	Looking for images online; on-screen annotations
Preparation	Make a list of the past simple and past participle of irregular verbs that you would like to review or introduce in class.

in class

1   Write this on the board: *sp...* Tell the students that these are the first letters of a very common irregular verb in English. Can they guess the verb? (e.g. *speak* or *spend*). What are the past simple and past participle forms?

2   If the students have a list of irregular verbs (on a previous handout or provided by the textbook), tell the students to choose ten irregular verbs and write the first two letters of their infinitive forms on a piece of paper. Then they switch papers with a partner and try to guess the verb and write the infinitive, past simple and past participle on the piece of paper they get from their partner. You may also write the first two letters of ten common irregular verbs on the board yourself. Tell them that if some partners are having difficulty guessing some verbs, they can add a third letter.

3   Now get or make a list of irregular verbs, open your Internet browser and run a search for the verb *speak* for instance, on Google, then click on "images". Have the class look at the prompted results. Now tell them that you are going to run another search and while you do that they should not look at the board. In the meantime open the "desktop annotate" tool in Activinspire or "transparent background" in Notebook or "screen annotation" in Mimio (or the equivalent tool from your companion software).

3   Run a search for an irregular verb on Google Images. Use the pen tool from the screen annotation menu and place a blotch of ink over anything that may give the word away (such as the typed verb itself on the search box) or over any inappropriate pictures. This should take just five or six seconds. When you are ready, tell the students they can look at the board again. In pairs and by looking at the pictures on the board, can they guess what the verb is? Give them a few seconds to discuss and then elicit answers.

4   Repeat step 3 with different verbs.

Variation 1

If you are not using a companion software or it doesn't include the screen annotation tool, you could use any of these free online annotation tools: bounce or diigo (see page 29).

1.18 *Speak, spoke, spoken*

Variation 2

Instead of looking for the pictures in class while the students look away, take screenshots of your picture searches at home and place each picture on a different page of the companion software (or the presentation software of your choice).

Variation 3

The preparation is a bit time-consuming but the advantage of multiple use with the same class or different classes in different years is considerable. Take about 24 screenshots of different image searches for the most common irregular verbs and copy and paste each resulting picture on a different page. Then ask the students to create a bingo card of 4x4 squares and write a different irregular verb on each square. Show the pages one by one with an interval of about ten seconds in between pages and, if the students think that the images they see match a verb they wrote, then they circle the verb. The first student to circle ten verbs wins, assuming:

a: they can also give you the past simple and past participle.

b: you confirm that the circled verbs match your image search.

Variation 4

This kind of activity is also very suitable for expressions with common delexical verbs, such as *take, get* or *give*. For instance, at a Pre-intermediate level the following image searches will provide interesting pictures that are not blatantly obvious: "get a job", "get an appointment", "get home", "get hurt", "get a deal", "get a message", "get a cold", "get a ticket", "get along".

At an Upper-intermediate to Advanced level you may introduce or review lexical chunks such as *Do you get what I'm saying?, get a whiff of, get a grip (on), get a life*. If the image search is not satisfactory because the images aren't very revealing try to google synonyms of those expressions. For instance, instead of *Do you get what I'm saying?*, google *understand* but ask the students to think about the target question rather than the word *understand*.

Follow-up

Ask the students to go online and look for about eight images that can illustrate irregular verbs. Then they can copy and paste those images onto a word processor. Ask them to print a copy and also save the file onto a pen drive, save it to online storage sites such as Dropbox or to notetaking and archiving sites such as Evernote. They can display the documents on the board (without the typed verbs) for the rest of the class to guess the verbs. Then they can decorate a wall in the classroom with the printed copies (and write with a marker the verbs next to the matching pictures).

Spot the difference

Focus	Grammar: Prepositions of place; *there is/there are*
Level	Beginner to Pre-intermediate
Time	10–15 minutes
ICT Skills	Copying and pasting images
Preparation	1 Take a photograph of a busy and very well-known street in your town where people walking by, shops, cars, traffic lights, trees or signs can be seen. Wait a minute or two and take another photograph from exactly the same spot and from the same angle.
	2 Upload both pictures to a blank page.

in class

1 Tell the class about the two photographs that you took this morning/last week, etc. Do they know the street? Do they frequent it? When are they there and what for? What kinds of shops are there? What can you buy in them? Are there any interesting landmarks? (at the suggested language level you may need to explain this word) How busy is it at this time in the morning/afternoon/evening?

2 Review with your students target grammar and language needed to describe and compare the pictures that you are about to show. Write these words and phrases on the board: *there is/there are/I can see/in the back/in the front/on the right/on the left/in the middle/behind/opposite/in picture A...; however, in picture B.../is walking/is crossing/is waiting*, etc.

3 Now display the page with the two pictures and give your students time to compare in pairs the two pictures and highlight the differences.

A

B

How many differences can you find?

Spot the difference

4   Elicit answers (e.g. *in picture A we can see a bus on the road but in picture B we can see cars and a motorbike. In picture A the young girl wearing a sweater is looking to her right but in picture B she is looking to her left. In picture A the short woman dressed in black is walking on the pavement but in picture B she is crossing the road on a red light, etc.*).

Variation 1

If you do not have time to take the photographs or you and your students do not live in or near a fair-sized town, try running an online search for pictures. You may try to find two different photographs from Times Square or Piccadilly Circus shot from the same angle.

Variation 2

For a more challenging experience place each picture on a different page instead. Leave the first picture for a minute or two and ask your students to try to remember as much as they can. Then display the second picture.

Variation 3

A slight variation from variation 2. When you display the first picture, tell your class that only Students A can look at the board. Then Students B can only look at the board when the second picture is shown. Finally show a blank page or turn off the projector momentarily and have the pairs of students work out the differences.

Follow-up

Now it's time for a few students to take their own pictures with their phones or cameras in the same fashion. Ask them to place the pictures on a slide in a presentation tool of your choice (e.g. Powerpoint/ Keynote/ Voicethread/ Prezi/ Emaze) and open those files from the computer in class for extra practice next day. In addition to street pictures, the students may also take pictures at home in their living rooms or bedrooms. In that case they will have to move things and make changes in the room right after they take the first picture (for instance they can place a pair of slippers on the floor, put some books on a table, get their dog or cat (if they have pets at home) in the picture, turn the TV on, etc.).

The tallest person in the world

Focus	Grammar: Superlatives
Level	Elementary to Intermediate
Time	15–20 minutes
ICT Skills	Copying and pasting images
Preparation	Choose a variety of adjectives for your students to practice the superlative forms and type them on a page. These adjectives work well for this activity:

big, small, polluted, tall, short, long, beautiful, ugly, good, bad, easy, difficult, dangerous, intelligent, safe, hot, cold, expensive, boring, exciting, comfortable, funny, interesting, popular, fast.

in class

1   Show the page listing the adjectives. Think of adjective and noun combinations for some of the adjectives on the page. For example you can say: *size, family, class, problem, question* for the students to say *big* or *small* or *river, sea, water, air* (*polluted*), or *person, tree, building* (*tall*). You can check for common combinations beforehand in a corpus-based tool on the Internet.

2   Now ask the students to take a blank A4 sized piece of paper and fold it three times so that they can get eight cards out of it. Ask them to cut out the cards along the folds by using scissors or their hands. Explain that you want them to practise forming superlative adjectives. Write this on the board: *the longest river in the world.* It will be their task to write similar phrases where a superlative form is followed by a noun that combines well with the adjective used (*the tallest building in the world, the most polluted sea in the world,* etc.). They must write one phrase per card. Four cards per student should be enough. Circulate to collect cards. It is not imperative that everyone gives you four cards. Collect, however, at least two cards from each student.

3   Now pick up a card and type the phrase written on it on Google with inverted commas. Click on "images". Ask the class to look at the pictures. Ask the students to work in pairs. Then pick up one card at a time and type what is written on it. The students guess what the phrase is by looking at the picture. It is very important that they only look at the board when you ask them to. Obviously, they cannot be looking at the board while you are typing the phrase.

4   Pick up a card and ask the students to look away or close their eyes. Type the phrase with inverted commas on Google Images and scroll down the page just enough to hide your search query from view. Tell the students they can look at the board now. Give them about 30 seconds to make their guesses. Depending on what the student wrote on that card, the prompted images will be very evident or not. Scroll up the page a bit so that the query can

be read. The first student in each group to have made the correct guess gets a point.

5   Follow step 4 with ten to fifteen more cards.

Variation 1

Instead of asking the students to produce the phrases, do it yourself before you see the students in class and take screenshots of the results. Copy and paste each screenshot onto a slide on a presentation tool of your choice (e.g. Powerpoint/ Keynote/ Voicethread/ Prezi/ Emaze) or a page on your IWB companion software and ask the students to guess what the superlative phrases are.

Variation 2

Run an online search for six to eight different phrases and copy and paste one image from each onto a slide on a presentation tool (e.g. Powerpoint/ Keynote/ Voicethread/ Prezi/ Emaze) or a page on your IWB companion software. Type the relevant adjectives for those six to eight search queries and include another four or five. Show the pictures and typed adjectives on the screen in class and ask the students to generate phrases and match them with the images.

Follow-up

Ask the students to look for various superlative phrases at home, print out pictures and bring them to class next day. They can use an A4 sized sheet of paper to print four different images illustrating an equal number of phrases. Once they print the pictures out, they must cut them out and write the phrases on the back. Collect all the cards and ask the students to work in groups of four or five. Distribute cards evenly amongst the groups and ask them to sit around a table and place the cards face up. Each student must take a piece of paper and write on it what they think the phrases written on the back of the cards are. Give them about two or three minutes. Then they can turn the cards over and check. Tell your groups to switch cards with other groups a few times.

Search for "the biggest country in the world"

1.21 Tag it

Focus	Vocabulary review
Level	All
Time	15–20 minutes
ICT Skills	Copying and pasting images
Preparation	1 Find a variety of images on the Internet with no specific search criterion, e.g. images of a jungle, a living room, a bus stop, a famous painting, some food, a football stadium, a book cover, a famous actress, a fish tank and a street rally.
	2 Place each picture on a different page, enlarging the size so that they take up most of the screen.

in class

1 Ask your students if they are familiar with the word *tag* in the context of labelling things on the Internet. For example, many bloggers tag their articles with key words that summarize the content of those articles. Sometimes users who upload pictures tag those pictures with key words as well so that they can be found in search engines when those words are typed.

2 Open the document that you created and, showing the first picture as an example, ask the students to think of appropriate tags or key words or phrases for it. For the picture of the jungle a group of students at an Elementary to Intermediate level may generate words such as *jungle, trees, leaves, green, Amazon, forest, rainforest, vegetation, explorer, nature*. Students at an Upper-intermediate to Advanced level may come up with the words above and other words such as *mahogany, deforestation, dense vegetation, tangled vegetation, cutting your way through, logging, liana, shrub, moist*.

3 Show the next picture. Each student takes a piece of paper and writes down as many words as they can think of to tag the picture, as in step 2. Give the students a couple of minutes to work individually. Then ask the students to work in pairs put their pens down and compare their word lists. How many words or phrases do they have in common? Elicit answers.

4 Follow step 3 with the remaining pictures.

Variation 1

For Advanced levels, run an image search with a given word such as "jungle" and then choose two or three similar pictures and place them on a page. What do the pictures have in common?

Variation 2

Ask students to work in groups of four. Each group will be made up of a pair of students competing against the other pair. Follow the lesson outline indicated above and then have each pair count how many words they have in common. The pair within each group with the highest number of word coincidences wins. Play a few rounds.

Variation 3

At the end of a textbook unit ask the students to look at the images accompanying the unit. Ask them not to use their notes and to try to hide from view the text on the pages by covering it with their hands or pieces of paper. Ask the students to tag the images, one at a time, as in the lesson outline. Hopefully they will be using some of the new vocabulary learnt and practised in the last few days. If you have a digital version of the textbook, draw attention to the pictures by enlarging them or by hiding the text around them and ask the students to tag them.

Follow-up

Choose a couple of pictures from the ones you have worked with in class. Ask the students to think of other words and phrases that could be adequate for tagging in L1 that they may not know in English. Tell them to use dictionaries at home, look those words up, write them down and bring them to class next day.

1.22 Textbook writers

Focus	Writing and speaking around a topic
Level	All
Time	35–45 minutes each session
ICT Skills	Creating a slide with a presentation tool (e.g. Powerpoint/ Keynote/ Voicethread/ Prezi/ Emaze); placing text and images; embedding a voice recording in it
Preparation	1 Look for an image that can be used to illustrate a topic that you want to cover in class. For example, you can look for a picture of a plane on the topic of travelling or a picture of a group of teenagers playing football on the topic of sports.
	2 Copy and paste the selected picture onto a blank page.

in class

Day 1

1   Ask the students to work in groups of three. Tell them that they are going to create a textbook page around a picture that you have chosen. Show the picture on the board.

2   Ask the following questions: *What can we see on the picture? What topic could the picture illustrate? What other alternative topics could it illustrate?* Elicit answers.

3   Now write these tasks on the board:

a. reading passage

b. listening extract (with questions)

c. conversation questions.

Each group member will have to choose a different task. If the number of students is not divisible by three and you have some students working in pairs, then those pairs will choose the first two tasks.

4   Each student gets pen and paper. They will be working in their groups but each task involves individual work. Thus the students working on a reading passage will have to write a reading passage of around 60–80 words of length that is somehow related to the topic illustrated by the picture. The students working on the listening extract will need to write a transcript of about 80–100 words and provide two to three listening comprehension questions about the transcript. Those working on the conversation questions will be providing four to six conversation questions on the topic. Early finishers (most likely those who have task c) may help out their peers in the group. Circulate to provide help and any necessary corrections or suggestions.

5   Collect all the papers, make corrections as necessary and hand them back in the next few days.

6 Explain that the members from each group will have to work collaboratively online outside school hours. They can go to a computer lab, a library or work from home. They could choose online tools such as Prezi, Animoto or Google Presentations or computer software such as Powerpoint or Keynote. Most students will be familiar with Powerpoint and will probably have that software installed. A free software option is Impress from Open Office. They will have to produce one document with two slides. The first one will contain a relevant image for the topic and the reading passage. The second slide will contain an embedded voice recording of the listening transcript, the listening comprehension questions and the conversation questions. The students can work separately, email their work and piece it together in one file or arrange to meet physically.

Day 2

7 The files are opened in class and the groups, in turns, display their work on the whiteboard and present it. Depending on time availability and class size, you may decide to fully play some of the voice recordings or engage the students in conversations around the questions. Give due credit to the students for both the group's final outcome and for each individual contribution.

Variation 1

You may decide to increase the number of students working in each group and, as a result, increase the number of tasks and slides in each presentation. Other additional tasks might be: creating and embedding a video, providing a list of useful words and expressions or creating a questionnaire.

Variation 2

Ask the students to go online and look for relevant material on the chosen topic at the target language level. Instead of producing texts and placing them on a slide they can simply provide the links.

Variation 3

Choose an interesting reading passage from a different textbook series to the one you are using and write key words and phrases from it on the board. Let the students create a meaningful text using as much of the vocabulary as they can.

Follow-up

Based on variation 2, you could set up a wiki for the class with as many pages as topics you will be covering during the school year. The students can then add relevant links with reading and listening material for those topics.

1.23 Texting

Focus	Vocabulary review
Level	All
Time	10 minutes
ICT Skills	Copying and pasting images
Preparation	1 Find eight pictures where you can see a variety of people in different settings. For instance, a crowded beach, an office, the front door of a cinema, a classroom, a crowded road, a shopping centre, a restaurant and a library. Place four of those pictures forming a column on the left hand side of a page and place the remaining four forming a column on the right hand side.
	2 Find a picture of a mobile phone and copy and paste it on the same page. Scale it down and make it considerably smaller than the pictures already placed on the page. Duplicate this picture. Place the two pictures of the mobile phone on the top.

in class

1 Open the document with the pictures in the last ten minutes of your lesson and direct the class attention to the board. Ask a student to choose a picture from the left and a picture from the right. It does not matter which ones they choose. Now drag the pictures of the mobile phones, place them over the chosen pictures and draw a line linking them.

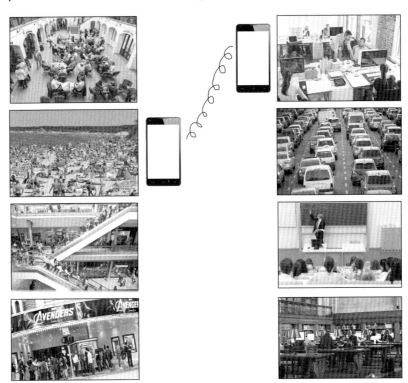

Talking and texting

2 Ask your class what kind of conversational exchanges on the phone two of the people from the selected pictures could be having. Who are those people? How do they know each other? What are they doing there? Why are they talking on the phone? What are they talking about? For example, any given person basking in the sun in the crowded beach and someone sitting at a desk in an office (*How are things in the office? Well, I'm having a nice time here on the beach. It's 24 degrees here, just wonderful. Coming back home from this nice break on Wednesday next week. See you at work then, etc.*).

3 Now ask the students to say some interesting words and expressions that they have seen during the teaching period. Elicit about eight words and expressions and write them in the space left in the middle of the screen. This time tell the class that the two people are exchanging text messages on the phone. They need to get a piece of paper and, in pairs, simulate a text chat between those two people. Their task is to write down short conversational text exchanges and use two of the words or phrases from the board. Give them about five minutes to do this. Circulate to provide help and possible corrections.

4 Invite the students to read their short written texts.

Variation 1

If there are enough Internet connected devices in the classroom the students can be engaged in real text chat from their mobile phones or laptops instead of using pen and paper.

Variation 2

Instead of choosing two pictures, let each pair of students decide which two pictures they want to work with. When they read their written dialogues, the rest of the students will have to guess which two pictures were chosen.

Variation 3

This activity presents itself well for drilling certain grammatical structures. For example, at an Advanced level it has proved useful to provide practice for unreal uses of past simple and past perfect with *I wish, I'd rather, If only, It's time.*

Follow-up

If you have a blog or wiki for the class, ask the students to upload those written dialogues. Then access them from time to time in class and highlight key vocabulary.

Too many cooks

Focus	Vocabulary for food, cooking and recipes
Level	Pre-intermediate to Intermediate
Time	30–40 minutes
ICT Skills	Copying and pasting images; grouping (optional)
Preparation	Find pictures online of food and spices and of cooking actions (stirring, frying, boiling, baking, seasoning, beating, draining, etc.). Your starting point could be a dish that you are familiar with. Then look for a recipe of that dish on the Internet and make a note of the ingredients and the cooking actions for that dish. Next run a search online for pictures of those ingredients and the cooking actions. Copy and paste the pictures onto a blank page. Look for a few extra pictures of food and spices and cooking actions that are not relevant to the dish in question. For instance you could place a total of 10–15 pictures that have a direct link with the dish and three or four distracters.

in class

1 Ask the students if they like cooking and if they are good at it. Ask: What can you cook? What's your favourite dish? What do you eat at home (cooked by themselves, their parents, flatmates, etc.) that you enjoy? You may also ask them other questions on the topic of cooking, such as:

- How can we learn how to cook? What's the best way?

- How did you learn to cook?

- What's the last meal that you cooked for yourself? How did you cook it? How did it go?

- Do you know dishes that are typical from other countries? Do you know the recipe?

- If you had a guest from another country who has never tried any Spanish/French/Italian/Russian (name your own country) dish, what would you cook for them?

2 Elicit vocabulary for cooking actions and ask a student to write down those words on the board.

3 Now show the document that you created with the pictures. Ask the students to work in pairs and tell their partners what they see and what the cooking verbs might be. If they have trouble seeing some of the pictures, enlarge them momentarily and then scale them down.

4 Invite a student to come up to the board and drag the pictures showing food and spices to the left and the ones that show cooking actions to the right. Invite more students to the front to write and label the pictures. Group each picture with the word/s (optional).

5   The students, working in pairs again, try to work out what the dish might be and also the recipe of it based on the pictures and the vocabulary on the board. Make sure you tell them that there are a few distracters. Give them a few minutes for this task and encourage them to come up to the board, drag the pictures and explain what the recipe is.

6   Finally reveal the dish that you had in mind and drag the relevant pictures in order as you explain the steps required to cook it.

Variation 1

Instead of using pictures, simply type the words on the board. It's a less powerful and less memorable alternative but the activity can be set up very quickly.

Variation 2

In step 5 ask the students to write down the recipe on a piece of paper in about 100 words. Then pin the papers on the classroom walls and ask the students to read the resulting recipes and vote on their favourite/most accurate ones.

Variation 3

In step 6 play a video of that recipe that you can find online instead of telling the recipe yourself.

Follow-up

Ask the students to look for a recipe online and take notes on the ingredients required for the dish and the cooking verbs. Then they look for relevant pictures that can illustrate the ingredients and the actions and they place them on a word processing document or slide of a presentation tool. (e.g. Voicethread/ Prezi/ Emaze) or Powerpoint document. Then they show the pictures on the board and let the class know about the dish and how it's cooked.

Ask if anyone would like to try to cook the dish that you showed on the board at home. They can take pictures of the cooking process and of the final result and show the class. They may even bring the dish to class, if they want to (and are allowed to).

1.25 Why?

Focus	Discussing art
Level	Upper-intermediate to Advanced
Time	25–35 minutes
ICT Skills	Browsing the Web; copying and pasting images
Preparation	Find an intriguing painting online that can prompt an interesting discussion around it in class. For this activity I have chosen Emily Mary Osborn's *Nameless and Friendless*, 1857. The painting shows a young woman artist who is offering a picture to a dealer in an attempt to sell her works. She is accompanied by her younger brother. Do some research on the painting and copy and paste a picture of it onto a slide in a presentation tool of your choice (e.g. Powerpoint/ Keynote/ Voicethread/ Prezi/ Emaze) or a page from your companion software. Here are some useful shortened links:

- http://www.tate.org.uk/art/artworks/osborn-nameless-and-friendless-the-rich-mans-wealth-is-his-strong-city-etc-proverbs-x-15-t12936 (short link: http://bit.ly/ZUEIF5): A description of the painting from the Tate website.

-http://smarthistory.khanacademy.org/emily-mary-osborn-nameless-and-friendless.html (short link: http://bit.ly/194GlCT): An interpretation of the painting from Khan Academy. Practically all the questions listed below find their answer in this link.

- http://en.wikipedia.org/wiki/Emily_Mary_Osborn (short link: http://bit.ly/15PK5H7): Wikipedia entry on Emily Mary Osborn.

Other paintings that might be used successfully for this kind of activity are:

- *The Arnolfini Portrait* by Jan Van Eyck

- *The Triumph of Death* by Pieter Bruegel the Elder

- *The Maids of Honour* by Velázquez

- *The Ambassadors* by Hans Holbein the Younger

- *Bathers at Asnières* by Seurat

- *Nighthawks* by Edward Hopper

- *An Experiment on a Bird in the Air Pump* by Joseph Wright

in class

1   Tell the class that you will be showing them a painting on the board and you want them to write down questions about it starting with *why*. They can think about and write as many questions as they wish. Give them about five or six minutes and circulate to provide help and make any necessary corrections. Here are many interesting questions for this painting (whose answers may be found in the links above):

1.25 Why?

- Why is the woman wearing a black dress?
- Why is she wearing a hood?
- Why isn't she wearing a ring?
- Why is she looking distressed?
- Why are her hands toying with a piece of string?
- Why is she looking down?
- Why is she standing and not sitting down on the empty chair?
- Why is she accompanied by a boy?
- Why is the boy holding a portfolio?
- Why are they inside an art gallery?
- Why is the bald man in the middle looking at a painting?
- Why does the bald man have his index finger on his chin?
- Why are the other men in the picture wearing top hats?
- Why aren't those men looking at the painting of a ballet dancer that one of them is holding?
- Why is there another woman and a child by the front door?
- Why are there so many paintings on the walls?
- Why is the name of the painting *Nameless and Friendless*?

2   Now ask the students to work in groups of five or six to have a look at their questions and discuss them in their groups.

3   Repeat step 2, this time in plenary mode.

4   Finally ask the students to write in about six to eight lines a description and a personal interpretation of the painting based on the ideas gathered so far. If you have written relevant lexis on the board, encourage them to use the words and expressions they have just learned.

5   Ask volunteer students to read out their written texts.

Variation 1

Write up a list of questions for them to discuss. However, this activity is much more engaging and richer if you let the students write the questions first and then perhaps you provide some additional questions based on your research on the painting.

Variation 2

Ask a student to choose a painting, do some research on it and show it on the board to the class. The rest of the students think of questions starting with *why* for this student to answer based on the findings.

1.25 Why?

Variation 3

If you have enough Internet connected devices in the classroom or you can take your class to a library or media center, give them the links listed above and ask them to find answers to the generated questions there immediately after step 3 of this activity.

Variation 4

Ask the students to do research on a painting. Then in class tell them to answer your *why*-based questions.

Follow-up

If you are unable to do Variation 3, ask the students to do it at home. They can then fine-tune their impressions and reflections. On a more general note you may ask them to spend some time online reading about Victorian times, as this particular painting is a manifestation of social life in 19th century Britain.

Acknowledgment: I learned this activity from Hania Kryszewska, who learned it from Bonnie Tsai.

CHAPTER 4 ACTIVITIES
4.2 SOUND AND VIDEO-BASED ACTIVITIES

A stroll in the city

Focus   Functional language: Giving directions

Level   Elementary to Pre-intermediate

Time   15–20 minutes

ICT Skills   Taking photos, copying and pasting images, board annotations, screen recorder tool

Preparation

1. Take some photographs of easily identifiable landmarks in your city (squares, museums, parks, a sports centre, a main shopping street, a shopping mall, an old church, the train station, etc.). Alternatively, ask your students to find those pictures online or search for those pictures yourself. Eight pictures is a good number.

2. Place those pictures on a blank page.

3. Open another page and place those pictures on the second page as well. Decrease their size and place them at the bottom of the screen. Then find a map of the city and copy and paste that map on this page. You can easily do so by typing "map of (name of city)" on your Web browser and following the link to Google Maps. Then you can use the zoom in/zoom out tool and the cursor to choose an area. Make sure that the map is placed on the bottom layer.

in class

1. Ask your students to work in pairs and brainstorm words for places in town. After a couple of minutes elicit answers.

2. Introduce (or review) key phrases for giving directions in English: *go straight on, go down the street, turn left/right into High Street, take the next/second/third street on the left, it's on the other side of the road*, etc. Elicit different ways of asking for directions: *Excuse me, how do I get to...?/Sorry to bother you but do you know the way to...?/Excuse me, can I just ask you something? Do you know where... is?/How do I get to...?* etc.

3. Open the first page of your document and bring any two pictures to the middle. Ask a student to give you directions from picture A to B. Repeat this a few more times with different students.

4. Now let the students, in pairs, choose pictures and give directions.

5. Open the second page. Ask a student to drag the pictures from the bottom of the screen and place them on the map.

6. Open the screen recorder tool and start a recording. Now ask a student to draw directions from one picture on the map to another with the pen tool, erase it, draw another line showing the way from one picture to another and erase this line, repeating this procedure three or four more times.

7. Play the recording and ask the students, in pairs and in turns, to narrate what's happening while trying to keep pace with the recording.

2.1 A stroll in the city

Variation 1

For an additional element of surprise, hide the pictures on the first page. This may be done in many different ways. This is a possible one: create a solid object the size of half the page. Place it at the bottom of the screen. Lock it and place it on the top layer. Now hide all the pictures behind this solid object. The pictures can now be dragged from behind this object but cannot be viewed until they "leave" the object.

Variation 2

If you have Google Earth installed in the computer connected to the data projector, you can ask students to show directions to different places in town and use the target expressions. Another interesting resource is Google Street View.

Follow-up

Ask some students to volunteer to record a video in the street using a smartphone. They can practise the target language seen in class while pretending they are asking for and giving directions. Then they can upload the video file to a pen drive or use online storage sites such as Dropbox, or online video recording tools (see Mailvu on page 24) and play the video from the computer in class.

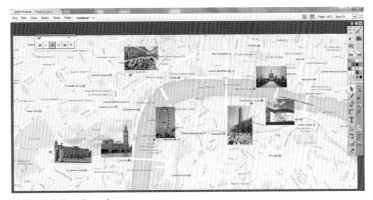

Map with landmarks

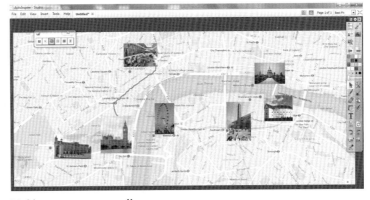

Making a screen recording

2.2 Advertising slogans

Focus	Critical thinking, language of advertising
Level	Intermediate to Advanced
Time	30–40 minutes
ICT Skills	Finding video clips of adverts; typing text
Preparation	1 Find some famous advertising slogans online. Choose a mix of slogans that your students will be familiar with and some others that they are unlikely to know. Some of the slogans should be intriguing and open to interpretation (for instance, *start me up*). Do not reveal the brand or company name. You can try googling "famous advertising slogans" or "famous commercial slogans". A very good source for slogans is www.thinkslogans.com. There is a list of selected slogans for this activity below. Type about 10 on a page.

2 Now find the video commercials of the selected slogans. This can be done by running this type of search query on a search engine or on YouTube: "start me up omega commercial". All the slogans provided for this activity can be found this way. Bookmark the links or copy and paste them on a document so they can be accessed easily in class.

Slogans	Companies
Start me up.	Omega
Childhood is calling.	Rice Krispies
Connecting people.	Nokia
Just Do It.	Nike
I'm lovin' it.	McDonald's
Everything we do is driven by you.	Ford
Because you're worth it.	L'Oreal
It's the real thing.	Coca Cola
Think different.	Apple
It keeps going, and going, and going.	Energizer Batteries
Be your way.	Burger King
You can do it. We can help.	The Home Depot
Gives you wings	Red Bull

in class

1 Ask students to work in groups of four or five and discuss these questions for about 5–10 minutes:
- What video commercials have you seen recently?
- What happens in them?
- Do they have slogans? If so, can you remember some?
- Which ones, in your opinion, are effective commercials and why?

2 Elicit answers from the groups. Play one or two of those commercials and have brief conversations about them.

3 Now open the document with the typed slogans. Ask the students if they can identify them and what kind of products they are trying

2.2 Advertising slogans

to promote. In most likelihood, most (if not all) the students will be familiar with McDonald's *I'm lovin' it*. Ask the following: *Why is the present continuous used rather than the present simple? Is there a difference in meaning?* Look at the remaining slogans and encourage critical thinking. Effective slogans usually carry more than one possible meaning. You may use *start me up* as an example and play the video (the commercial was aired just before the start of the London Olympics/to start a race/to start up a watch/The Rolling Stone's "Start me Up" song is played). What other meanings can be hidden behind the slogans they know?

4   Now tell the class to focus on the slogans they are not familiar with. Hopefully there should be at least one from the suggested list that they can't identify. What might be advertised under them?

5   Choose one slogan from 4. The students, in their groups, agree on a product being advertised with that slogan and write a short text including the slogan to promote it.

6   The groups read out their adverts.

7   Now play the video for that product. Did anyone guess the type of product? Were they surprised? Do they think it's a good commercial? Why? Why not?

Variation 1

As a lead-in for the activity, look for a different set of slogans on the suggested site above. Select a number of slogans that equals half the number of students you have in class (for instance, if you have 22 students, select 11; if you have 28, select 14; if you have an uneven number of students, get involved as a student yourself). Get strips of paper and write on them those slogans and the products separately. Give each student a strip of paper and ask them to stand up, mingle and find the matching partner.

Variation 2

Based on the video that the students have watched, ask them to, in their groups, think of a short alternative script and slogan for it. Assign enough time for the task and then play the video again with no sound and have the groups read their scripts in turns.

Follow-up

As work extension, ask the students to look for advertising slogans on the Internet. They should choose two slogans: one that should be easily identified by the classmates and one that they are not likely to know. They share the slogans with the class next day and have conversations around them.

Students could also produce commercials based on these slogans with their smartphones.

2.3 Bingo

Focus	Vocabulary for food
Level	Beginner to Elementary
Time	15–25 minutes
ICT Skills	Using a webcam
Preparation	Make a list of approximately 25 words related to food, such as fruits, vegetables, meals, etc. Type those words on a blank page.

in class

1   Open the document that you created and review the words with your class. This is a good activity in combination with textbook material dealing with this vocabulary set.

2   Now give each student an index card. If you have few students in class, give out more than one card per student. You can also make out cards from scrap paper.

3   Assign each student a different word from the board (Student A=orange, Student B=banana, Student C=potatoes, Student D=salad, etc.). Tell them to remember their words. There should be about 25 words in total. Some students may be assigned more than one word and card if there are fewer than 25 students in class. If there are more than 25, you can skip a few students or increase the number of words to 30–35. You can always adjust the number of words displayed on the board by adding or deleting some, as needed.

4   Tell the students that you are going to give them a couple of minutes to draw the assigned word on the card. Collect the cards from them.

5   Now ask them to get a piece of paper, draw a bingo card with twelve squares and write any word from the board on them (a total of 12 words).

6   Open the webcam and start your game of bingo by choosing any of the cards and placing it in front of the camera for the students to see on the board. Wait three or four seconds and place a different card in front of the camera. The students cross out from their bingo cards the words that match the pictures that appear on the board. The first student to cross out all the words in his card wins the game.

2.3 Bingo

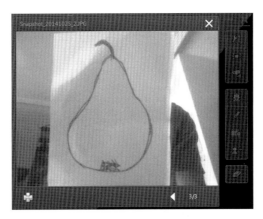

It's "p" for pear

7 Ask the students to draw another bingo card with different words and play another round.

Variation 1

Children may enjoy drawing in their bingo cards. In this case, instead or writing 12 food words, the students draw those words in their cards. The webcam will not then be needed for the activity. Simply call out and erase the typed words from the board, one at a time, for the students to cross out their drawings if they match the corresponding words.

Variation 2

You may want to play bingo with other vocabulary sets that are relevant for the suggested language level. It is important that those words are relatively easy to draw and to identify (body parts, clothes, places in town, house objects, free time activities, etc.).

Follow-up

Ask the students to create bingo cards with custom images. They can google "picture bingo card generator" and select one of the many websites listed to create free cards. Then they can print out a few bingo cards and bring them to class for another game of bingo.

Bugging fly

Focus	Grammar: Prepositions of place; Vocabulary for furniture and household objects
Level	Beginner to Elementary
Time	15–25 minutes
ICT Skills	Using the screen recorder from the companion software or an online screen recorder; layering objects
Preparation	Find a picture of a fly online and copy and paste it onto a blank page. Scale it down as much as possible and drag it to the bottom left corner of the screen.

in class

1   Review with your students vocabulary for house equipment. Ask them: *What furniture can we typically find in a bedroom/ a kitchen/ a living room? What household objects are usually found in these rooms?* You may elicit answers from them in plenary mode or give them some time to write them down and then ask them to say them aloud.

2   Review prepositions of place with materials at their disposal, such as the textbook, workbook or a handout.

3   Now open the document that you created. Tell your class that they are going to turn this blank page into a living room. Invite students to come up to the board and draw objects (a coffee table, a dining table, some chairs, a TV, some shelves, some books, a standing lamp, a couch, a heater, a rug, etc.).

4   Change the layering of some of the drawings. By default, annotations, such as drawings, go to the top layer and objects, such as the picture you copied and pasted, go to the middle layer. Change three or four drawings to the middle and bottom layer.

5   Now select the picture of the fly on the bottom left corner and enlarge it. Invite a student to come up to the board and drag it anywhere so that it is on/in/near/under/above/in front of/ behind/next to an object drawn on the page. Ask the class: *Where is the fly?* Ask the student to place the fly somewhere else now. Ask where the fly is now. Repeat this a few times.

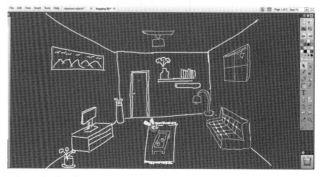

Where is the fly?

6   Open your companion software screencast recorder tool or an online screen recorder application. Make a recording of the fly being dragged on the screen and being dropped in different places. You, or a student, can drag it slowly it and place it on/in/near/etc. an object for about three seconds, then drag it somewhere else and so on.

7   Play the resulting video and ask the students to work in pairs and make sentences (*The fly is on the TV/The fly is behind the couch now/*etc.).

Variation 1

To speed this activity up, copy and paste a picture of a living room and skip steps 3 and 4 above.

Variation 2

1   Give a student a crumpled paper ball and invite him to place it in different places in the class for the students to construct sentences with prepositions of place (e.g. *It is in the dustbin/by the door/on the teacher's desk*).

2   Now record a video with a camcorder or a smartphone of those actions. Tell a student to do step 1 slowly, then ask someone else to grab the paper ball to do similar actions but a bit faster and finally ask a third student to do those actions considerably faster. A highly recommended tool for this variation is Mailvu app for Android or iPhones. You can make a recording with a smartphone connected to the Internet and then type the short link for the video on the main computer in the classroom to watch the video recording straight away. Ask the students to generate sentences using the prepositions of place. Play the video again pausing it at times to check answers.

Follow-up

Invite students to make their own recordings at home with online video recording sites (such as Mailvu). As they make their recordings they should also be saying what is happening (*The pencil case is on the coffee table, now it's under the table,* etc.). Play a couple of those recordings in class without sound first for the students to describe the actions and then with sound.

2.5

Clear your throats

Focus	Reading aloud
Level	Beginner to Intermediate
Time	10–15 minutes
ICT Skills	Using voice recording tools

Preparation

1 Choose a short reading passage (or an extract from a long one) from your textbook that you have already seen in class with your students or from a previous handout.

2 Open a voice recording tool and start reading the text. Make a few deliberate mistakes while doing so. For instance, for a text of about eight lines, mispronounce about five words.

3 Save your recording in a memory stick. Alternatively, use an online voice recording tool, such as Vocaroo or Voki, so that you can open the link in class to play the recording.

4 Select a different reading passage that the students have not read yet.

in class

1 Ask the students to locate the reading passage in their textbooks (or hand out copies of the reading passage).

2 Tell the students that you will be playing a recording of the text. There is a are a few mispronounced words (you may give them the exact number). It's their task to follow the recording and the text and underline the mispronounced words.

3 Ask the students to compare their underlined words with those of a partner and elicit answers.

4 Hand out the new reading passage (or tell the students to turn to the relevant page in their textbooks).

5 Choose a student to read the first two or three lines. Before she starts doing so, tell the rest of the students that every time they detect a pronunciation mistake, they should clear their throats out loud. Mispronounce a word yourself, such as *pilot* (you can say /ˈpiːlət/). Encourage the students to clear their throats. Tell them that you are going to mispronounce this word one more time and invite them to clear their throats even louder this time.

6 Now that the students are familiar with the procedure, have the first student read her part. If mistakes are made, the students should be clearing their throats when they hear each mispronounced word. When that happens, the student should stop reading for correction.

7 Repeat step 6 with other students until the reading passage has been read.

Clear your throats

Variation 1

For Beginner to Elementary levels you may make recordings of numbers or the alphabet. Introduce one mistake (for example, say "one, two, three, four, six, five... or a, b, c, d, e, f, j, h, i, g, k...). Use an online recording tool, send the link to the students and ask them to detect the mistake as homework.

Variation 2

Ask the students to use an online recording tool and to make recordings with "false definitions". They should provide definitions for words recently seen in class. Each recording could have five words with their corresponding definitions. Ask the students to include one false definition. At an Elementary level, this type of activity works well with words for family. For instance, *your cousin is your sister's son.*

Follow-up

Encourage the students to read texts out loud at home and make voice recordings with online tools or with their mobile phones and then listen to them. They can also make voice recordings of word lists and listen to them from time to time for consolidation.

Countable or uncountable?

Focus	Grammar and Listening practice; Dictation; Countable and uncountable nouns
Level	Beginner to Pre-intermediate
Time	10–15 minutes
ICT Skills	Using online video conferencing tools
Preparation	1 Get in touch with a class of students whose native language is English and who are learning your students' native language. The further resources section in this book offers useful information on finding other classes internationally.

2 Before the videoconference with your partner class takes place, hold a videoconference with the partner teacher. That way you can test the video conferencing tool (see page 23) and decide what kind of activity you would like your students to do as well as its time length. Agree on a day and time to meet.

3 In this hypothetical case, let us assume that the partner students, a Beginners class, are learning the months in German. Your students, a Pre-intermediate class, are practising the concept of countable and uncountable nouns applied to food and drink.

The underlying idea is that, at precise moments in the lesson, the students can collaborate and interact online and co-teach as well.

in class

1 Do any activities related to countable/uncountable nouns from your textbook, workbook or handouts that they students may have. Alternatively (or in addition to it), ask the students to draw on paper a table with two rows and two columns. They should write "countable" in the top row on the left and "uncountable" in the top row on the right. The bottom rows should be big enough for them to place about eight words in each.

2 Now dictate the words below (in any order). The students should place those words in the table according to whether they are countable or uncountable. The first eight could be listed, in principle, as countable and the remaining ones as uncountable (there are other alternative ways of placing them on the table).

potato, carrot, egg, watermelon, apple, strawberry, cucumber, fish, juice, bread, cheese, pasta, butter, meat, coffee, fruit

3 Elicit answers from the students and challenge some of their choices. Promote critical thinking. Are there any words that could be both countable and uncountable? In which ways can some of the uncountable words be made countable? (a *slice of/a piece of/a pound of/a chunk of cheese, bread, meat; a carton of/a bottle of/a glass of/a jug of juice*). Is it correct to say *a meat/two meats? How about a coffee/two coffees?* Why?

2.6 Countable or uncountable?

4   Go online and have a videoconference with your partner class. Ask your students to draw another table. Ask the partner students to call out words for food and drink for your students to place on their tables. If they hear any words that they encountered in the previous activity, they can leave them out. Keep a record of those words on a piece of paper to check understanding.

5   Now it's time for your students to do something for the partner class. They have been learning the months in German and their teacher is asking your students to make up sentences in German and articulate them slowly and clearly for them to copy down. For example they can think of facts or things that are true of themselves and incorporate the words for the months, as in the examples below:

Student A: - *Ich bin im Oktober geboren.*

Student B: - *Weihnachten ist im Dezember.*

Student C: - *Mein Lieblingsmonat ist Juli, weil ich da Urlaub habe.*

Student D: - *Mein Lieblingsmonat ist August, weil meine Eltern da ein Ferienapartment auf Mallorca mieten und wir dann eine Woche gemeinsam verbringen.*

Student E: - *Februar ist der kürzeste Monat des Jahres.*

For practical purposes I am showing these two examples of interactions that can take place among the students but it may be anything that is agreed by the participating teachers.

6   Go offline. Each teacher will go over the tasks with his/her students, check understanding and provide feedback. For instance, you can highlight grammar points derived from the sentences or check accurate spelling or do pronunciation work.

Variation 1

An activity that works well for higher language levels (Intermediate to Advanced) is descriptions and discussions around a picture. Both teachers choose the same picture for their classes. The students have conversations around the picture in L2. Then the classes go online and the students have similar conversations in L1, which is a considerably easier task but an invaluable source of authentic and tailor-made listening material for both classes. Write down useful vocabulary and expressions and review this with your students once you go offline. If you have a programme installed in your computer that can record streaming audio, such as Audacity, make an audio recording of your partner class. After you have reviewed some of the vocabulary, play the recording. Alternatively, make this recording available to your students by posting it to a blog or wiki or by emailing it to them.

 Countable or uncountable?

Variation 2

If you teach children, you can agree on a song to sing or a performance, such as a dance, or ask the students to bring artifacts that are representative of their region, culture or country.

Variation 3

Establish a calendar for the classes to meet regularly. A suggested meeting frequency is every three weeks for about 10-15 minutes. The students can then exchange conversations in the target languages.

Variation 4

Establish a partnership with another English classroom in your country (or even in your school). Meet every three weeks and encourage conversations in English. You could even set up a quiz with questions to test their knowledge of English.

Follow-up

Ask the students to write on paper or on a blog their impressions on these kinds of interactions. Encourage them to add suggestions for future types of activities.

2.7 Fragmented listening

Focus	Listening practice; Grammar: Third conditional
Level	Intermediate
Time	15–20 minutes
ICT Skills	Using voice recording tools, inserting sound files

Preparation

1 Select a grammar drill exercise from the students' textbook, workbook or from a handout. In our case we will be choosing an exercise from *For Real Intermediate*, Martyn Hobbs and Julia Starr Keddle, Helbling Languages, page 206, that drills the use of the conditional. The exercise includes a solved example and nine items.

1 Rianna's friends weren't at the party, so she didn't stay long. If Rianna's friends had been at the party, <u>she would have stayed longer.</u>

2 I didn't know you were coming, that's why I went out. If I _____ you were coming, I _____ out. (etc)

2 Choose the first five items, as solved in the answer key. Open a voice recording tool such as the voice recorder included in Windows, Audacity, the online voice recorder Vocaroo or the voice recording tool from your IWB companion software (this last option is the easiest). Make ten separate voice recordings from the chosen items. Each item will be broken down into two recordings; one for the *if*-clause and the other one for the main clause. For instance, you would make two recordings for item one: *if Rianna's friends had been at the party* and *she would have stayed longer.*

3 Place the icons for the recordings on a blank page in any order.

4 Get five additional items from another source (or make up your own). Follow step two but this time place the icons for the *if*-clauses on the left hand side of the screen and the icons for the main clauses on the right hand side of a new page.

in class

1 Ask your students to complete the sentences from the exercise and then go over the answers with them.

2 Now open the document with the recordings and invite a student to come up to the front. Explain that she will have to click on the icons until she finds two matching halves. When that happens, she can drag the icons and place them next to each other on a corner of the screen. Invite a second student to find two other matching halves and so on.

3 Once all the matching halves have been pieced together, open the second page of your document. This time they will have to match other fragmented conditional sentences but it will be a slightly different, and a bit more challenging activity, as they are

not familiar with these sentences. Invite a student to come to the front and click on any icon on the left and all of the icons on the right. He should wait for each recording to play fully before he is ready to click on the next one. Ask the students to listen and write down on paper the matching halves.

4   Elicit answers and confirm the correct combination.

5   Repeat this procedure with the remaining recordings.

Variation 1

You could try this activity with many other grammar points e.g. question making, the present perfect (make sure that the auxiliary *have/has* and the participle are placed on separate recordings), zero, first, second and mixed conditionals, passive, modal verbs (again the modal verbs and the main verbs should be placed in separate recordings), comparisons.

Variation 2

You can also use this activity for language chunks rather than grammar. Here are some examples for the word *way*:

- *By the way,... how's your brother doing?*
- *This is way... too expensive for me.*
- *There is no way... I'm going to pay 10 euros for this.*
- *Is there any way... I can help you with this?*

If there is more than one possible combination, then ask your students to work out the best matches.

Variation 3

You can also make fragmented recordings of proverbs or idioms for the students to match.

Follow-up

Ask volunteer students to create fragmented recordings. They can place them on a slide in Powerpoint (insert>sound>sound from file) and then email the Powerpoint document to their classmates. The students can open the documents at home, drag the icons for the sound files and place them together.

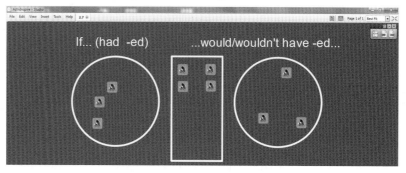

Screenshot with the embedded audio recordings

2.8 Get it?

Focus	Delexical verbs: Expressions with *get*
Level	Pre-intermediate to Intermediate
Time	20–30 minutes
ICT Skills	Using a webcam
Preparation	Select about 15–20 expressions with *get* that are adequate for the suggested language level. Your adopted textbook will most likely provide some expressions or you may use the ones here:

get home, get to work/school, get to (London), get older, get to know, get on well with, get married, get divorced, get angry, get dark, get tired, get lost, get better/worse, get a text message' get a present, get a job, get hotter/colder, get off the bus/train, get late

in class

1   Teach the vocabulary and let the students practise. You may take these expressions from the textbook and use the teaching ideas and materials provided by it. You may ask the students to translate the expressions into their mother tongue and write a few sentences that are general truths or true of themselves, such as *When I get home, I turn my computer on and check my emails/I get to school by bus/I get on well with Damien/It gets hotter in summer/The economy is getting worse*, etc. You can also create some conversation questions for the students to discuss in small groups and then in plenary mode (*How do you get home?/How do you get to school?/Do you get tired in this class?/When was the last time you got angry? What happened?/What was the last present you got?* etc.).

2   Now ask each student to get a blank A-4 sized piece of paper and fold it three times so that they can get eight cards out of it. Ask them to cut out the cards along the folds by using scissors or their hands. There will have to write one expression with *get* on one side of each card. Tell them to turn the cards over.

3   Ask the students to work in groups of four. In turns, they will have to convey the expression written on any given card through drawing in the space on the back of the card where they wrote the expression. Quite obviously, they have to hide from view the written expressions. You may want to ask your students if they are familiar with the game Pictionary, as this activity is based on this game. You can also type "how to play Pictionary" on YouTube and choose and play a short video.

4   Give the students about eight to ten minutes to draw and guess the expressions. Each group should first quickly agree on which rules they are going to have before they start drawing.

5   Now collect about two or three cards from each student. Open the webcam or in-built camera of your computer and place one of the cards in front of the camera. The students will see it greatly magnified on the board. Ask the class what they think the expression is (the student who drew it and the students in her group will have to remain silent). Do the rest for the remaining cards.

6   Finally choose about 15 cards (you can use the same cards you used before or get new cards from the students). Record a short film with the webcam where you show a drawing for about six to eight seconds and then you flip the card so that the written expression will be revealed. Follow these steps for the remaining cards. The students will have six to eight seconds to call out the expressions when you play the video.

Variation 1

Choose other expressions with *get* that are suitable for Upper-intermediate to Advanced levels (*get cold feet, get away with, get by, get your own back, get rid of, get a life, get a kick out of something, get into something, get your act together, get your teeth into something, get out of my face, get real, get the picture, get a whiff, get the sack*).

Variation 2

You can adopt this activity to teach other lexical items such as lexical sets, idioms or phrasal verbs.

Variation 3

Save the last ten minutes of your lesson and ask your students to choose two or three interesting words or expressions that they have learned today. Ask them to draw them on a piece of paper and then use the webcam for the whole class to see and recall.

Follow-up

Do not throw away the cards. Keep at least one card from each expression, stack them and keep them in the classroom. Do this for any other lexical items where you ask your students to draw. Then recycle this lexis from time to time by means of the webcam and the board.

Invite the students to create their own videos with drawings at home or with their mobile phones. Ask them to use online applications such as Mailvu or Eyejot. Then they can share the links and play the videos from their classmates outside school and you may also play some videos in class.

Guest speaker

Focus	Listening practice
Level	Elementary to Intermediate
Time	10–15 minutes
ICT Skills	Recording, transferring and retrieving videos or recording videos with online tools and clicking on links to play them (recommended)
Preparation	Ask a native speaker of English or a fluent speaker to record a short video of about two minutes of length. In this video this guest speaker could provide some information about his hobbies in life, what he does for a living and what he has been up to lately. This video can be recorded with the camera and software installed in his computer and then emailed to you or stored in online storage sites such as Wetransfer or Dropbox or uploaded to YouTube as a private video. However, I strongly recommend using online recording tools, such as Mailvu or Eyejot.

in class

1   Ask your students if they know and keep in touch with native speakers of English. Where do they live? How did they meet each other? How do they communicate? How often? Do they use text messaging? Do they exchange emails? Are they friends in social networking sites such as Facebook? Do they do videochats on Skype?

2   Tell the class that they are going to watch a video recording of a personal presentation from a friend/acquaintance of yours. You may share how you know each other and reveal a couple of things from the recording.

3   Ask the students to get a piece of paper and draw a table with three sections: Hobbies, Occupation, Lately. At the suggested language level you may need to explain the meaning of the adverb *lately*. It is their task to write as much information as they can in the relevant boxes when you play the video.

4   Play the video once and then let the students compare their notes with a partner.

5   Play the video again. This time you may select the on-screen annotation mode and write key words and phrases from the recording on the sides of the screen as the video is playing.

6   Elicit answers from your students. Draw attention to the board annotations for the students to provide details about them.

7   Ask the students to write down one question they would like to ask your guest speaker from what they've just found out about him. The whole class will have to choose the most interesting six to eight questions.

8   Email your guest speaker the questions for a second video.

Guest speaker

Variation 1

Preview the video and prepare a set of eight to ten True/False statements based on the information provided by the guest speaker. Dictate the statements to the students or write them on the board for them to copy. The students watch the video and decide which of the statements are true and which are false.

Variation 2

Summarize the content of the video recording before you play it and also add two or three inaccuracies. The students should listen to you but not take notes. Then let the students watch the video and decide what the inaccuracies are.

Variation 3

This time the students bring a guest speaker to class. Preview the video beforehand and prepare a set of True/False statements.

Variation 4

Adapt this activity for Upper-intermediate to Advanced levels by asking your contact to provide more specific information. It would be a good idea to send him some questions beforehand and let him know about the language level of the students.

Follow-up

Train your students on how to use online recording applications, such as Mailvu or Eyejot, and encourage them to record their own videos with personal presentations. They may invite their classmates to watch those videos by sharing the private links with them.

If the video is available online, ask the students to provide a full written transcript of the first minute. They can play the video at home and pause it and rewind it as many times as needed. Review the transcripts with the students and play the video next day in class.

How do you say it?

Focus	Pronunciation: Individual words
Level	All
Time	15–20 minutes
ICT Skills	Accessing online dictionaries
Preparation	None

in class

1. Write on the board four or five challenging words for the language level you are teaching that some of your students might have trouble pronouncing correctly.

2. Ask a few students to say those words aloud. Correct any possible mispronunciations.

3. Now ask the students to work in groups of thre. Each student will be assigned a portion of their textbook. For instance, if you have just covered one or two units, assign evenly the pages from that unit or units. If you have covered three units, each student will be assigned one unit (this activity works better if you have covered at least three units). If you have covered more than three units, divide the number of pages by three and give each student their share of pages.

4. Tell the students to scan for and choose five challenging words from their assigned unit/s (or pages within a given unit). They should look for words that they find particularly difficult to pronounce. They have no more than five minutes to do so. Ask them to write down those words on a piece of paper.

5. The students now share what they wrote on paper with their group members on the desk and ask each other to pronounce those words. If they are not sure about the pronunciation, they want to contest it or they think that the word has been mispronounced, they should raise their hand and show you the word.

6. Each time a student shows you a word, access an online dictionary that provides pronunciation, such as howjsay (www.howjsay.com) or forvo (www.forvo.com). Type the word, click on it and let the students hear it.

This activity is quite suitable as a way to start or finish a class.

Variation 1

If your students have Internet connected devices in the classroom, such as smartphones, tablets or laptops, let them access the online dictionaries instead. One device per group would be enough. You may decide to set up larger groups of four to five students so that the ratio is one device per four to five students.

Variation 2

Some digital versions of textbooks incorporate pronunciation of some key content words (most commonly in the vocabulary section). In this case you may want to use your digital textbook instead of an online dictionary.

Follow-up

Encourage your students to download dictionary apps on their phones. At the time of writing this page provides some good information: http://appadvice.com/appguides/show/english-dictionary-apps (shortened link: http://bit.ly/afWMBr).

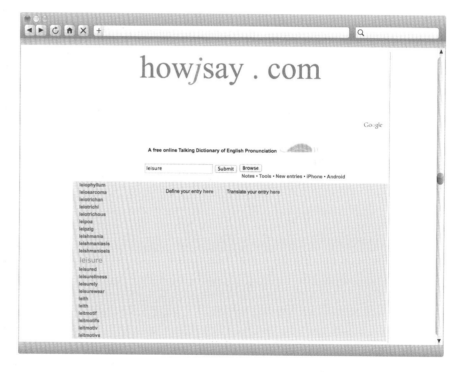

A search for *leisure* on Howjsay

2.11

It's all in the news

Focus	Listening practice: news stories on video; Writing news stories around key lexical items
Level	Intermediate to Advanced
Time	30–40 minutes
ICT Skills	Looking for video clips online; embedding videos (optional)

Preparation

1 Look for two news stories online of between one and a half and two minutes long. These stories should have a completely different nature. For instance, a sport story and an international news story. The portal www.cnn.com provides ideal stories for this kind of activity. Go to that site and then click on "video" on the top menu. Then you will see categorized news stories. You may download and embed those videos onto a page from your companion software or just simply play those videos from the Internet.

2 Preview the videos and select key vocabulary (about six words or phrases from each video). Type this on a page in no particular order.

3 As an option select about four to six headlines from different sections of an online newspaper and type them on a page.

in class

1 Ask the students to name sections from radio or television news broadcasts or from newspapers. As an example here are the different sections provided by The Guardian online: News, Sport, Comment, Culture, Business, Money, Life & Style, Travel, Environment, Tech, TV, Video, Dating, Offers, Jobs. Once you have elicited answers from the students you may want to go online and have a quick look at the headlines on the front page.

2 In addition to step 1, show the page with the typed headlines from the newspaper. Ask the students to decide in which sections they would place those headlines. These are real examples taken from the Guardian digital edition on 30 Dec 2012 (the actual sections are in brackets). You can use these headlines (bear in mind that this edition may not be available when you are reading this) or those from today's paper.
- QPR vs Liverpool – live! (Sports)
- Lucy Porter: What inspires my standup routines (Culture)
- Beat the British chill and head west (Jobs)
- Single men found to be rubbish at putting out the recycling (Environment)
- New activities on the French slopes (Travel)

Ask the students to justify their choices. There are no wrong or right answers as long as they can provide a plausible explanation. You may want to draw attention to key vocabulary ("standup" as in *standup comedy* or *comedian*; therefore probably Culture). To make it easier provide the words for the sections as well for them to match.

3   Show the page with the jumbled-up words and phrases from the two video stories and ask the students to copy them down on paper. Tell them that you will be playing the first twenty seconds of two news stories on video for them to get acquainted to some extent with the stories. Then they will have to decide which words and phrases might go with the first story and which ones go with the second story based on the understanding they have gained so far. Next they will have to choose one story and write it down in about three or four lines.

4   Circulate to help students and invite them to read their stories.

5   Play the stories and ask questions to test understanding. Provide extra vocabulary and phrases that are relevant and interesting for the language level. Play the videos again.

Variation 1

A less challenging variation would be to simply choose one news story and ask the students to work around the target vocabulary and phrases provided.

Variation 2

If you have enough Internet connected devices in the classroom or language lab, ask the students to access the Sky News website and click on "Watch the latest 3m bulletin" or look for "one-minute world news" on the BBC site. Give them a few minutes to watch the news bulletin and take notes of string of words that they can understand (of no less than four words coming together). They may pause and rewind the videos if they want to. Next invite them to come up to the board and write those phrases in any order (eight to ten is a good number). Finally tell the students to drag and place the phrases in order to match the various news stories.

Follow-up

If you decide to include step 2 in your lesson, ask the students to choose headlines from different sections of an online newspaper as homework. They should write them down on the front of a piece of paper and write them again on the back with the corresponding section in brackets. They bring them to class and switch papers with classmates. When they are ready to check answers, they can turn over the paper. You could assign six to seven minutes for them to switch papers as many times as they can within this given time. In the likely scenario of having more students than papers, the students can then work in groups of three or four.

2.12

Lips don't lie

Focus	Pronunciation: Minimal pairs
Level	Beginner to Intermediate
Time	10–15 minutes
ICT Skills	Recording videos with a webcam or the laptop's in-built camera
Preparation	1 Select sets of minimal pairs (pairs of words that only differ in one sound, for instance *cat* and *cut*) that are relevant for your class. English learners whose native language is Spanish tend to have difficulty discriminating the sounds /b/ and /v/. Italian learners of English find trouble with the sounds /æ/ and /e/ Here are some examples for these sets.

berry/very   sad/said   boat/vote   bad/bed

ban/van   land/lend   bet/vet   had/head

2 Open your camera software programme and place yourself really close to the front of the webcam or camera lens of your laptop in such a way that it captures a close-up of your nose, mouth and jaw.

3 Record the selected words. It could be just one recording with a two-second gap in between words or a separate recording for each word or set of words. If you are making these recordings with a different computer from the one you have in class, make sure you save them in a memory stick.

in class

1 Write *minimal pairs* on the board. Ask the students if they know what this means. It's fine if the students explain this in their mother tongue for the suggested language levels. If nobody knows, explain what this means yourself.

2 Write down the two phonetic symbols that you want to do contrastive work on and ask the students to think of words that have those sounds. Alternatively, write a couple of examples of words that contain those sounds underlining the letter/s involved to make things easier for the students. Write on the board the accurate words suggested by the students.

3 Drill the words and raise awareness of the features of these sounds.

/b/ lips are closed, voiced

/v/ the upper teeth make light contact with the lower lip, voiced

/æ/ mouth slightly more open, front of the tongue raised just below the half-open position, lips neutrally open

/e/ front of the tongue raised between the half-open and half-close positions, lips loosely spread

4   Play the video recordings. The students will be able to see the position of the lips and teeth in great detail.

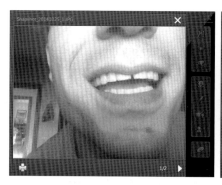
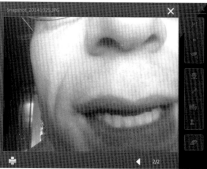

sad   said

Variation 1

All textbooks have regular sections of pronunciation in the units. Sometimes they focus on contrastive pairs, sometimes on individual sounds, other times on sound clusters or connected speech. In addition to the activities provided by the textbook you could make (at home or in class while teaching) recordings of those drills, then invite students to come up to the front and make recordings themselves.

Variation 2

Focusing this time on vocabulary review, make a video recording of about ten words that your students have seen in class recently. Leave a gap of about four seconds in between words. Articulate those words clearly. Then play the recording in class with the sound off and ask the students to write down what they can see on a piece of paper. Elicit answers. Then play the recording again with sound to confirm those answers.

Follow-up

Ask for 10–15 volunteer students to make this type of video recordings at home using online video recording sites such as Mailvu or Eyejot. Give each participating student a piece of paper with a word or expression that they have recently seen in class. They will have to create a sentence of their own (or get an example from a monolingual dictionary) containing that word or expression. They should articulate the words well. As in variation 2, play those videos in class, one at a time, with the sound off and ask the students to guess. This time a context will have been provided for the focal lexical items. Play the recordings again with sound.

2.13 Literal video version

Focus	Writing texts to match moving images
Level	Intermediate to Advanced
Time	15–20 minutes for Day 1; 15–20 minutes for Day 2
ICT Skills	Browsing the Web; using voice recording tools and online screen recorders (optional)
Preparation	Browse a few "literal video versions". Literal video versions are parodies of popular music video clips where the creators of these videos combine the video footage from the video clip with their own made-up lyrics that try to describe what's happening in the video (sung to the tune of the song usually with added subtitles). You can find information on literal video versions here: http://en.wikipedia.org/wiki/Literal_music_video. Simply type "literal video versions" on YouTube to browse some videos. Three videos worth watching are the spoofs on *Take on Me* by A-Ha, *You are Beautiful* by James Blunt and *Total Eclipse of the Heart* by Bonnie Tyler. Choose one video for the class.

in class

Day 1

1 Ask the students if they are familiar with mash-up videos (videos which are made out of different media such as different video sources, sound snippets, images, etc.) What examples of mash-up videos do they know? (political satires, movie trailers, lipdubs, literal video versions). Ask now if they are familiar with literal video versions. If so, invite those students that may know to explain what they are. Do they know a funny one?

2 Play the literal video version that you have selected for the class.

3 Now ask your students to think of music video clips that would present themselves well for a literal video version. If they are not very sure, run a search for "best music video clips of 2014" online, preview about 30 seconds of three or four videos and tell the students to choose one.

4 If you have enough Internet connecting devices in the classroom, follow the steps below for Day 2. Otherwise, give the task for the students to do at home. They should focus on the first minute of the selected video clip, and write alternative lyrics for it, as they have just seen with the video you played earlier. They will obviously need to pause and rewind the video repeatedly. It is up to them to provide alternative lyrics for the entire video if they want.

2.13 Literal video version

Day 2

1 Ask the students to work in groups of four or five and share out the texts that they have written. Each group must nominate their favourite alternative lyrics.

2 Invite the nominees from each group to read out their lyrics. This time the entire class must choose a winner.

3 Play the video clip with no sound and ask the winning student to read out her alternative lyrics while trying to keep pace of what's happening on the screen.

Variation 1

Take about eight to ten screenshots of the video footage and place them on a page in no particular order. If the video has subtitles, place a blotch of ink over the subtitles on the resulting pictures. Play the literal video version, minimize the Internet browser and ask the students to listen to the song, look at the pictures and arrange them in order.

Variation 2

Instead of a song, ask the students to provide an alternative script for a movie trailer or a short (60 second) extract from a film.

Follow-up

Introduce the concept of screen recording to the class, if they are not familiar with it yet. Show them a couple of online screen recorders, such as Screencast-o-matic or Screenr. Ask volunteer students to produce a literal video version with either the lyrics they chose earlier or their own. They would have to play the video with muted sound and do a screen recording incorporating their voice.

2.14 Making comics

Focus	Functional language: Giving advice/making suggestions
Level	Pre-intermediate to Intermediate
Time	20–25 minutes for Day 1; 10–15 minutes for Day 2; 10–15 minutes for Day 3
ICT Skills	Using online comic creators (recommended site: www.dvolver.com; alternatives are www.toondoo.com, www.wittycomics.com); creating screencasts (recommended site: www.screencast-o-matic.com; alternatives are www.screenr.com, www.screenbird.com)
Preparation	1 This activity involves the use of online comic creators and online screencasting tools. The recommended tools are DVolver and Screencast-O-Matic. Get familiar with using them so that you can introduce them to your class of students.

2 Open a page from your companion software or a slide in Powerpoint. Type the following on the right-hand side:

- How about *-ing*?
- Why don't you...?
- You could...
- I'll tell you what, ...
- You should...
- You might want to...

Type the following on the left-hand side:
- ... is trying to learn a new language.
- ... is spending a year abroad to ...
- ... wants to go on a date with you.
- You have a friend who...

in class

Day 1

1 Start off your lesson but all of a sudden, get your mobile phone out and pretend to read a text message that you have just received. Pull a quizzical look. Now tell your students that you are sorry about this distraction but a close friend needs your advice. Make up a situation or use this one: one of my friends has an extraordinarily intelligent eighteen-year-old daughter who doesn't feel like studying at University because she plays the bass for a rock band. Playing for this band involves a lot of travelling. The band is ready to launch their first album and they are convinced they are going to get famous. Her father, however, does not see eye to eye (you may need to explain this expression). He wants my opinion on this. To be honest with you, I'm not sure myself. What would you do? What would you say? Who do you identify with more?

2   Invite the students to make suggestions. Write useful phrases and structures on the board. Elicit other phrases and structures for giving advice or making suggestions. Write them on the board as well.

3   Now open the document that you created and review the phrases on the right-hand side.

4   Focus the students' attention to the left-hand side of the board. Ask them to work in pairs and complete the sentences logically to create situations. For instance, for the first item: *My best friend/ My boyfriend/My father/My grandmother is trying to learn a new language.* Elicit complete sentences from the students.

5   Now, in pairs again, ask them to play roles. Student A reads a completed situation for Student B to give advice using the structures from the board. Then they can switch roles.

6   In plenary mode invite students to read out situations and advice.

Day 2

Access www.dvolver.com and show the students how to create a comic. Give them the task to select one of the situations and create a basic dialogue featuring a situation and advice/ suggestion. Each student should email the resulting comic to himself/herself. Once they have done this, tell them to use the screencasting tool Screencast-O-Matic to, in pairs, create a screen recording of the comic incorporating their voices. Then they can share the generated URL with the class for everyone to watch.

Day 3

Take a look at the comics in class.

Variation 1

For Upper-intermediate levels you may want to introduce additional structures, such as *I'd better...* or *... is worth a try.*

Variation 2

Adapt this for other functions, e.g. apologizing, agreeing and disagreeing, accepting or turning down invitations, making plans.

Variation 3

Ask the students to create comics using language chunks they have just been exposed to.

Follow-up

Have a school comic competition with other classes and ask the students to post the generated URLs in a blog or wiki.

2.15 Minimal pairs

Focus	Pronunciation: Minimal pairs
Level	Beginner to Elementary
Time	5–10 minutes
ICT Skills	Browsing the Web

Preparation

1 As in activity 2.12, select sets of minimal pairs (pairs of words that only differ in one sound, for instance *cat* and *cut*) that are relevant for your class. This time we will focus on ɪ/iː (*sheep/ship; eat/it; heat/hit; leave/live; reach/rich; leap/lip; seek/sick*)

2 Access the online pronouncing dictionary www.howjsay.com to get familiar with its use. As an alternative site, you may also use www.forvo.com.

in class

1 Write *minimal pairs* on the board. Ask the students if they know what this means. It's fine if the students explain this in their mother tongue. If nobody knows, explain what this means yourself.

2 Write down the two phonetic symbols that you want to do contrastive work on /ɪ/iː/ and ask the students to think of words with those sounds. Write on the board the accurate words suggested by the students. Drill the words and raise awareness of the features of these sounds.

3 Now access www.howjsay.com and type in the text box the sets of minimal pairs. Each word must be followed by a semicolon mark (*sheep;ship;eat;it;* etc.). You will now see the words you typed listed in a column. Every time you hover over a word with the mouse, you will hear it pronounced. Hover over a different word at a time and ask the students to repeat.

Wordlist created on Howjsay

2.15 Minimal pairs

4   Tell the students to work in pairs, get a piece of paper each and ask them not to look at the board. You may also turn the projector off momentarily or, better still, hold down the Fn key of your computer and press F5 (or the appropriate function key at the top of the keyboard) to change the projection mode to computer screen only. Make sure the speakers are on. Hover over a word for the students to write down the word they hear. Confirm.

5   Repeat step 4 with the remaining words. You may hover over the same words more than once.

Variation 1

Tell the students to take a sheet of paper and write /ɪ/ on one side and /i:/ on the other side taking up most of the space. Hover over a word on the board while they are looking down. Then tell them to look up and hold their sheets of paper up in the air showing the relevant phonetic symbol. Repeat this with all the words written on the board in no particular order.

Variation 2

Create odd-one-out activities. Type *rich;people;women;sit* and ask the students to listen to the words without looking at the board to let you know what the odd word is. This could be a sound awareness activity, as in the example above, or a lexis/word recognition-based activity as in: *wardrobe;shelves;armchair;socks*.

Follow-up

If the media player Real Player (www.real.com) is installed in the computer, the sound clips can be downloaded by right-clicking on the word and choosing the "download this video" option from the pull-down menu (it will actually download as mp3). The pronouncing dictionary Forvo (www.forvo.com) allows users the download of the sound clips by simply clicking on the word and then choosing the "download as mp3" option. Show this in class to your students and then encourage them to, in addition to keeping written vocabulary lists, compile "vocabulary sound albums". They can then place these mp3 files in folders and download them to their mp3 players or smartphones for vocabulary review.

A wiki for the class can be created (see activity 3.25 Wikidictionary) where both written form and pronunciation of the words can be incorporated.

2.16 News leak

Focus	Writing news stories from key focal vocabulary; Listening practice
Level	Intermediate to Advanced
Time	20–30 minutes
ICT Skills	Playing videos; typing text
Preparation	1 Find a news story on video of about two to three minutes. The video section of www.cnn.com offers a wide array of news clips that are appropriate for this type of activity. Alternatively you may also find news stories on http://news.sky.com (scroll down and find videos on "video timeline") or www.bbc.co.uk/news/uk (click on "video" on the upper menu).

2 While you are watching the selected video, write down on a piece of paper about 10–12 key words and expressions from it.

3 Type about seven or eight of those words and expressions on a blank page. Open another blank page and type about seven or eight words and phrases, including about three or four that are displayed on the previous page and another three or four that are not. This is an example of key words and phrases from a news story covered by CNN about a lawsuit for $67 million filed against two Korean immigrants in the USA who owned a dry cleaning business and who lost a pair of trousers.

Page 1	Page 2
- a pair of pants	- a pair of pants
- $67 million	- $67 million
- laundry business	- laundry business
- better education for our children	- attorney
- received a letter from the Court	- everything fell apart
- at first very happy	- United States of America
- American dream	- May 1992

in class

1 Tell the class that they are about to watch a news story but before they do that, you are going to leak some key information and they will have to construct a feasible story out of it. Remind them that it's not at all important if their story coincides with the video you selected for them. Reveal first the words in common from both pages (in the example above *a pair of pants, $67 million and laundry business*). Give the students a couple of minutes to confer with a classmate and then elicit some answers.

2   Ask students to work in pairs (Student A and Student B). Tell the class that you are going to display two sets of extra key words for the story. When you display the first set, only Students A will be allowed to look at the board and write down the words. When all Students A have copied down the information on a piece of paper, you will display the second set. This time only Students B will be looking at the board and copying down the words. When they have finished copying, open a new blank page.

3   The students work individually now and reformulate their guesses with the new extra information. They share their guesses in pairs.

4   Now they are allowed to look at each other's notes and reformulate for the last time. They should come up with a feasible story using their combined notes. Elicit possible news stories from the pairs of students.

5   Now play the videoclip for the students to compare. Ask questions about the video and check understanding.

Variation 1

Record a short video telling an anecdote and play it in class, instead of using a news story. Make sure that you provide key words and expressions beforehand and that you use them when you tell the anecdote. Play the video a second time and pause it from time to time to direct attention to the key words and expressions.

Variation 2

You may just use one set of words instead of two, which will shorten the activity to 15–20 minutes. In my experience, however, the main activity is conducive to more creativity and overall engagement in addition to more student output.

Follow-up

Ask the students to go online, watch the video at home, take notes and write a summary of it in about 50–80 words.

2.17 One word at a time

Focus	Reading: Retrieving words and language chunks from texts
Level	All
Time	10–15 minutes
ICT Skills	Using the screen recorder from the companion software or an online screen recorder

Preparation

1   Choose a reading passage from the Internet or from your textbook for your students to read in class and do work on. You can devise reading comprehension based activities or follow or adapt the text exploitation provided. A text of about 150 words is ideal for this activity (not necessarily for the text exploitation). For a longer text, either break it down into different sections and place it on different pages or just select the first 150 words. Copy and paste or type the text.

2   Select the pen tool and place a blotch of ink over each word, except for the first one. If you have more than one page with text, do the same with all the pages.

3   Now open the screen recorder tool from your companion software or access an online screen recorder (my recommended Internet tool is Screencast-O-Matic but you may also use Screenr or Screenbird).

4   Start a recording. Select the eraser tool. Erase the first word that is covered with ink, read it out, wait about three or four seconds, then erase the next word, wait about another three or four seconds and read it out. Follow this process until all the words have been unveiled and read out.

5   Print out copies of this text for the students. You will not need to do this if you have chosen a text from your textbook.

in class

1   Follow or adapt the text exploitation provided or devise your own activities to go with the text.

2   Write *one … at a time* on the board. Ask the students to suggest words that can fit the gap (e.g. *step, person, thing, card, word*). Ask them What do these expressions mean? What does *one word at a time* mean?

3   Open the document that you created and ask the students to work in pairs or threes. Tell them about the recording that you made. Explain that when you play the recording the covered words will gradually be unveiled with a pause of three to four seconds in between words. The students will have to try, in turns, to retrieve each word before it is revealed. They get a point for each successful attempt (they can just make a mark on a piece of paper each time this happens). The winner is the student with the highest number of retrieved words before they are displayed on the board.

2.17 One word at a time

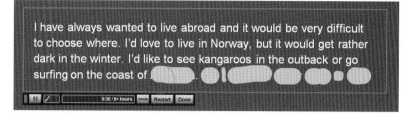

Screencast with Screencast-O-Matic

4   Ask how many points the students got.

5   Underline interesting language chunks from the text.

Variation 1

This activity can also be done without making a previous recording. You would just display the text with the words covered in blotches of ink, stand at the front and reveal the words, one at a time every three or four seconds, with the eraser tool. The recording, however, allows you mobility in the classroom and also unobstructed view of the text for the students.

Variation 2

An extra challenge would be provided by placing one blotch of ink covering whole language chunks. Thus *one word at a time*, for instance, would be covered by one longer blotch of ink rather than five individual ones over each word.

Variation 3

You can apply this principle to isolated sentences as well, focusing on vocabulary. Also, you can type grammar exercises from your textbook or workbook and cover the target grammar words for your students to retrieve within the time constraint given.

Follow-up

If you used an online recording tool such as Screencast-O-Matic, you can ask the students to try this one more time on their own by accessing the link to the recording.

Encourage the students to use this technique and challenge themselves to retrieve words. It's not essential that they have the technology that you used to cover the words in digital ink or that they block from view every single word from a text or a sentence. They can focus on isolated interesting grammar words or language chunks by simply copying down gapped texts on a piece of paper.

Phone messages

Focus	Grammar: Reported speech
Level	Intermediate to Upper-intermediate
Time	30–40 minutes
ICT Skills	Uploading voice recordings
Preparation	Draw a 4x4 table that takes about ¾ of the screen with the verbs below (in any order)

deny	invite	offer	ask
tell	decide	promise	agree
insist	apologize	suggest	hope
warn	remind	recommend	threaten

in class

1   Write the following questions on the board:

- How many different messaging tools/programmes/systems can you think of? (letter, voicemail, email, SMS, WhatsApp, Viber, Line, Skype, Facebook, Twitter, etc.)

- Which one/s do you use the most? What are the advantages/disadvantages?

2   Now give the students about 5–10 minutes to discuss these questions in groups of four to six and then elicit answers in plenary mode. Ask other follow-up questions to interact with the students' output.

3   Ask these questions and invite volunteer students to answer.

- *When was the last time you left someone a message?*

- *What messaging tool/programme/system did you use?*

- *What did you say or what did you write?* (if this is not too personal).

4   Now ask students to get some paper and write down on it a hypothetical message that they would like to leave on someone's phone. You can write some examples on the board of a reminder, a suggestion/invitation and a request (*Don't forget to meet me at 8 o'clock just outside Sounds Good Records. / Going dancing tonight? / Can you please help me with my homework? I'm online*). Give them a couple of minutes to do this and circulate in the meantime to correct possible mistakes and to provide help. Each student should write at least one message.

5   Open the page of the document that you created and the voice recording tool of your IWB companion software. Invite your

students to come, one at a time, and record their messages. Each message should be a separate recording. Place the resulting audio icons outside the table. If you teach a small class (15 students or fewer), ask the students to make two recordings each. To avoid having idle students you may ask the class to complete work on reported speech from their textbooks or workbooks or a handout while the recordings are being made.

6   Now divide the class into two large groups: A and B (boys vs. girls or students born in January–June vs. students born in July–December). Ask a student to come up to the front and click on any audio icon for the students to listen. Any student from his group may then tell him to drag this icon and place it over a word from the table and generate a reported speech sentence introduced by the reporting verb. For the first example above in step 5 the audio icon could be placed over the word *remind* and any student from group A could say *Ebba reminded Gustav to meet her at eight o'clock just outside Sounds Good Records.* If the generated sentence is correct, they can then write A on that square.

7   Now it's B's turn. A student from that team goes up to the front and clicks on another audio icon for any team member to generate a valid reported speech sentence using any of the left over reporting verbs from the table. If the sentence is correct, they write B on that square.

8   Now tell your class that the first team to get four As or Bs in a row (vertical, horizontal or diagonal) wins the game.

9   When the first game is over, drag away the icons, shuffle them and start a new game. This time team B starts.

Variation 1

For a shorter version, provide a 3x3 table with nine reporting verbs instead of 12 and play the original three-in-a-row.

Variation 2

Rather than creating the table at home beforehand, elicit common reporting verbs from your students and create the table in the classroom with their answers.

Follow-up

Create a private chat room in TodaysMeet and invite your students to type one or two messages there outside class hours. Open the chat room the following day in class and ask the students to report them (orally or in writing). If you have a wiki or a blog, you can use any of these platforms instead.

2.19

Put the headphones on

Focus	Listening practice
Level	Intermediate to Advanced
Time	15–20 minutes
ICT Skills	Finding video clips online
Preparation	1 Find a news story on video that does not exceed three minutes. The audio and video news section from the BBC or the video section from CNN (www.cnn.com/video) provide very good material for this activity.
	2 Preview the video and write down key vocabulary for the story and words that students may not know.
	3 Make sure you bring a pair of headphones to class.

in class

1 Welcome your students with a greeting (*Good morning/afternoon/ evening. How are you today?*). Articulate this utterance clearly but without producing any sound. Simply lip say it. Ask the class if they know what you have just articulated.

2 Encourage students to do this with words they have recently seen in class. They can stand up or, better still, come to the front and face their classmates so that they can be seen more clearly.

3 Now ask a student with a high level of English to come up to the front. Tell the class that this student will watch and hear a news story that you will be showing on the board. The rest of the class will watch the moving images on the screen but they won't be able to hear anything as you will be connecting a pair of headphones to the computer. Only the student in front will be able to hear the story through the headphones.

4 Now the class will ask the student in front 10–15 questions about the video. The first six to eight questions should be *Yes/ No* questions. Tell the student to provide accurate answers for the remaining questions but without revealing too much. If what she's being asked is not contained in the video, she can say *I don't know*. You can always clarify information if the student did not understand something in particular or is not too sure about it (or if she is providing wrong information).

5 Ask the students to work in pairs and write the story in about four or five lines with the information they have obtained from the video and the student.

6 Ask the students to read out their stories.

7 Now play the news story again with sound on for the students to compare.

Put the headphones on

8   Ask each pair of students to discuss what was right, what was wrong and what was missing from their predictions.

Variation 1

Ask students to work in groups of four or five. Ask each group to designate one student that will remain in class to watch the video. Ask the rest of the students to leave the class momentarily while the designated students watch the video. Then let the students in. Each designated student will be in charge of answering questions from their classmates in the group.

Variation 2

Ask one student to leave the room while the rest of the students watch the video. This student will then be asking questions about the video for the rest of the students to answer.

Follow-up

Provide the link for a news story on video for your students to watch after school hours. Then, in class, ask for understanding. Play the video in class and pause it from time to time to note vocabulary or check comprehension.

Questions for a video clip

Focus	Writing questions
Level	Elementary to Intermediate
Time	20–25 minutes
ICT Skills	Playing videos
Preparation	Find a music video clip containing a wide variety of situations, people and actions. For this activity the moving images should take priority over the music and the lyrics. You may run a search online with the words "the best music videos of all time" or "best music videos of 2014". This activity works well with the video clip of *Paradise* by Coldplay at an Intermediate level with satisfactory results. Other possible video clips you may use are *Take on Me* by A-Ha, *Girls just want to have fun* by Cindy Lauper and *If I Were a Boy* by Beyoncé.

in class

1 Write these questions on the board and let your students discuss them in groups.

- Do you like music video clips?

- Where do you watch them? On TV? On your computer? On your phone?

- What makes a good music video clip?

- Do you have any favourite music video clips? Which ones? What is good about them?

2 In plenary mode elicit answers from your students.

3 Ask the students to get a blank A4 sized piece of paper each and fold it several times so that they can obtain eight smaller pieces of paper out of it. Tell them to use six pieces. On each one, they should write a question about the video footage from a music video clip that you are about to play on one side and its corresponding answer on the reverse. They should concentrate on what is happening rather than on the music or the lyrics. If the video lasts about three minutes, they should ideally write a couple of questions for the first minute or so, another two for the next minute and a final two for the last minute.

4 Play the video and circulate to provide help or correct mistakes.

5 Collect all the cards from the students (it's not essential that all the students have written six questions and answers).

6 Ask students to work in groups of four or five and distribute all the cards among the groups. The cards should be dealt so that the side with the question on it is showing. Tell the students to place the cards on the table and not to turn them over. If there are cards that share the same question, they should only keep one of that kind and remove the others.

Questions for a video clip

7   Ask the students to number the cards by writing a number on the top right corner of each card. They should look at the cards and correct any possible mistakes. If they are not sure, they can always call you for help or confirmation.

8   Each student now gets a piece of paper and lists down as many numbers as numbered cards placed on the table. Within the group but working individually they write down on their papers the answers to the questions written on the cards. Set a time limit of about six minutes.

9   The students turn over the cards and check the answers.

10 Play the video a second time and explain that his activity was not about testing their ability to remember and recall actions from the video but rather about forming questions.

Variation 1

Music video clips present themselves well for this type of activity but you may find alternative video material that can be suitable as well, such as short stories or even video footage from your textbook.

Variation 2

Instead of getting the students into groups, use post-its (or pieces of paper and blu tack) and have them pin these pieces of paper to the walls of the classroom. Number them and ask them to stand up and move around the classroom and write down the answers on individual sheets of paper.

Follow-up

Ask the students to watch the video clip at home again and write a 50–100 word account of what happens in it.

Ask the students to have a critical look at the videoclip and analyse the images, the protagonists, the main message, colours and topics, for instance.

Ready for test

Focus	Speaking: Test practice
Level	All
Time	35–45 minutes
ICT Skills	Using online video recording tools

Preparation

1   Choose a general topic that you are currently discussing in class or that your students are expected to talk about in a speaking test. For instance, at an Intermediate to Upper-intermediate level, choose this topic: the media. Think of two or three relevant questions for this general topic, such as: *How have media changed over the last years? How relevant have media become for our society? How has technology affected the way we receive news? Do you trust the media?*

2   Access an online video recording tool, such as Mailvu (www.mailvu.com), Eyejot (www.eyejot.com) or www.videomessageonline.com and make a video recording with voice of about two minutes of length answering one of the questions. Alternatively, you can ask an English speaker to do this for you.

in class

1   Prepare a set of conversation questions for the class. You can run a search online with the query "esl conversation questions the media", use other sources at your disposal, such as the textbook, or create your own questions.

2   Better still, ask the students to work in groups of four or six and ask them to generate a set of three to six questions per group related to the topic. Tell each group to write down their questions on a piece of paper. Give them about five minutes to do this.

3   Now give the groups about six to eight minutes to discuss the questions written on the papers. Be flexible with time, as they may need more or less time depending on their level of engagement. Then ask the groups to swap papers so that each group receives a different set of questions. Allow about five minutes for group discussion this time. If there are questions that are the same as the ones discussed earlier, they can be skipped. Tell the groups to swap papers one last time for a further five minutes of language practice. While the students are engaged in these discussions, circulate to provide help or to suggest accurate language. Write useful vocabulary on the board.

4   Now in plenary mode, direct the students' attention to the vocabulary written on the board and clarify and contextualize the meaning. Invite a few students to share out their views on some of the questions generated.

5   Show the video that you created addressing the question *How have media changed over the last years?* or an alternative video with a question of your own choice. Pause the video from time to time to highlight useful expressions and good examples of speaking competency.

6   Now ask the students to choose any of the questions discussed in class and make, outside the classroom, a video recording of similar length and nature to the one they have just watched. Ask them to use an online video recording tool and email you the link so that you can watch the resulting videos at home and give them feedback.

7   Select a video recording that is a good example of speaking competency and play it next day in class, pausing it and drawing attention to good language use, as in step 5.

Variation 1

Instead of making the video recording yourself, ask a student to make one to show in class beforehand.

Variation 2

If the students are reluctant to make videos, ask them to use a video recording tool but place a piece of paper, such as a post-it, in front of the camera. That way the recording will capture the voice but not the image. Otherwise, they can also use online voice recording sites, such as Vocaroo.

Follow-up

Encourage the students to create voice or video recordings at home and try to incorporate the emergent language generated in class. Then they can play those videos, watch them critically and take note of weakness areas that they discuss with you.

Remember

Focus	Delexical verbs: Expressions with *give*
Level	Intermediate to Upper-intermediate
Time	20–25 minutes
ICT Skills	Using a webcam or an in-built camera
Preparation	None

in class

1   Tell your students that they are going to learn/review with you some expressions with the verb *give* including some phrasal verbs. Elicit some expressions from them and write them on the board.

2   Invite the students to make full sentences using the words on the board.

3   Add a few more expressions with *give*. A total number of 12–15 works well for this activity. You may select the ones given here:

give way, not to give a damn, give (it) a try, give rise to, give or take, give up, give in, give a sigh, give a ring, give a lift, give a shout, give off (a smell), give a signal, give away (an answer), something's got to give

4   Go through the expressions and explain the meaning. If the students have access to online or paper dictionaries, allow some time for them to look them up as needed.

5   Now ask your students to get a blank A4 sized piece of paper and fold it three times so that they can get eight cards out of it. Ask them to cut out the cards along the folds by using scissors or their hands. They will have to write one expression with *give* on one side of each card.

6   Now ask them to try to convey the meaning of each expression written on the cards on the other side through drawing. It will be easier in some cases than in others but reassure them that imagination, creativity and resourcefulness are more important and helpful than drawing skills. Assign about seven to eight minutes to do so. At that point tell the students to stop drawing even if they still have two or three cards remaining to draw.

7   Ask the students to work in pairs and place the cards on the tables showing the drawings. Do they have any matching cards? (drawings that make reference to the same expression). Ask them to exchange cards with other pairs and see if they can guess what the expressions are.

8   Now collect a total of 20 random cards from various students. If you have fewer than 20 students, pick up more than one card from a few students. If you have more than 20, give priority to your weaker students and start picking up cards from them.

Remember

9   Ask the students write the numbers 1–20 on a piece of paper. You will be placing the chosen cards, one by one, in front of the camera for them to see the drawings enlarged on the board with an interval of three to four seconds between cards. Say *card number one* out loud and place it in front of the camera. The students will then see a card with a drawing in it and will have three to four seconds to write down the expression that goes with it. Do the same for the remaining cards.

10 Repeat step 9 starting with your first card but this time asking the students what they think the expression was (the student who drew that card shouldn't give this away). Confirm by turning over the card and showing the written expression. Do the same with the remaining cards.

Variation 1

This type of activity is ideal for students to draw irregular verbs at an Elementary to Intermediate level or to draw situations with verbs in the present continuous at a Beginner to Elementary level. It also works very well for vocabulary sets at this last level (body parts, clothes, food and drink, furniture, places in town, jobs). At an Intermediate to Advanced level you may also use it for idioms and phrasal verbs.

Variation 2

Ask the students to work in groups of three or four and use some of their cards to create a story. For instance, Student A starts saying: *Last night Maria gave Pedro a call because she had something important to ask.* (Student A places the card with the expression *give a call* on the table.) Then any other student in the group can continue the story in a logical way and place an additional card on the table.

Follow-up

Invite the students to take their cards home and create video recordings with their mobile phones, tablets or laptops. They can place the cards one by one in front of the camera, as in step 9 in this activity. It works best if they use online video recording tools, like Mailvu. Then they can share the links and watch each other's videos and guess the expressions.

Song to sing

Focus	Listening practice
Level	Elementary to Intermediate
Time	20–25 minutes
ICT Skills	Voice recorder application

Preparation

1. Look for a song that you would like to play in class that is appropriate for the students' language level. The following sites feature songs (and lesson plans) for the EFL classroom:

   - www.isabelperez.com/songs

   - www.musicalenglishlessons.org

   - www.tefltunes.com

   - www.facebook.com (look for "Songs for Teaching")

2. Create a gap fill exercise with the lyrics and make copies for the class.

3. Two or three days before the day you're intending to play the song in class, ask for a volunteer to record his/her voice while singing a song. This recording can be made either in class just before or after school hours, or at home. For this recording you will need to plug in the headphones into the computer and open a voice recorder application such as the online tools Vocaroo (www.vocaroo.com), Recordmp3 (www.recordmp3.org) or Audacity (a free download from www.audacity.sourceforge. net). Make sure that the source for the voice recorder is set to microphone and not to the computer soundcard; that way the computer will record your student's voice and not the sound of the song. Give the volunteer student a printed copy of the lyrics and underline the parts that you would like him/her to sing (the words just before and just after the gaps on the students' handout). Start recording and play the song for the student to listen to through the headphones while looking at the copy of the lyrics. When the song reaches an underlined part, the student will have to sing just what's underlined on the paper. This is an example of an extract from the song *We are the Champions* by Queen. The underlined parts show what the student would be singing (and recording). Therefore when you play the recording in class the students will hear the volunteer student singing *I've paid my dues* followed by silence for four seconds, then *I've done my sentence* followed by silence for seven seconds and so on.

I've .... my dues	I've paid my dues
Time after time	Time after time
I've .... my sentence	I've done my sentence
But committed no crime	But committed no crime

2.23 Song to sing

And bad mistakes	And bad mistakes
I've .... a few	<u>I've made a few</u>
I've .... my share of sand	<u>I've had my share of sand</u>
Kicked in my face	Kicked in my face
But I've .... through	<u>But I've come through</u>
And I need to go on and on	And I need to go on and on

in class

1 Give each student a handout with the gapped words. Depending on the nature of the song (underlying topic, vocabulary, music style, etc.) devise a lead-in activity.

2 Play the song once for the students to fill in the missing words.

3 Let the students check answers with other classmates and elicit answers. It's likely that there will be some errors or troublesome gaps with no definite answers yet.

4 Now play the recording made by the student. This time it will be considerably easier for the students to understand what's missing.

5 Elicit answers again and, if the students are up to it, play the song and have everyone join in and sing it.

Variation 1

Give the volunteer student a copy with gaps in underlined lines. For example, in the extract used as an example above:

<u>I've .... my dues</u>	Time after time
<u>I've .... my sentence</u>	But committed no crime
And bad mistakes	<u>I've .... a few</u>
<u>I've .... my share of sand</u>	Kicked in my face
<u>But I've .... through</u>	And I need to go on and on

Follow the same procedure as in preparation 3. This time the volunteer student will sing the underlined parts without saying the gapped word.

In class, play the recording made by the student first. At this point do not hand out any printed copies of the lyrics. The students listen to the recording, write down what they hear and try to fit in suitable words for the gaps. Students compare their notes. Elicit answers. Then distribute the handouts and play the song.

2.23 Song to sing

Variation 2

Get the students to sing the song. Divide the class into two large groups: A (the students sitting to your left) and B (the students sitting to your right). Have the A students sing the uneven lines and the B students sing the even ones. Play the part of a conductor who cues the singers for extra fun.

Follow-up

Encourage your students to look for songs they enjoy or that are popular at the moment and bring the recordings to class for you to prepare a fill in the gaps listening activity.

They can also search for versions of songs on YouTube with lyrics. They play the video clip, sing along (and record their voices in the process). Then they can listen to the recording at home and get a feel for how they sound in English.

2.24 Sound clips

Focus	Writing narratives
Level	Beginner to Intermediate
Time	40–60 minutes
ICT Skills	Downloading and embedding sound clips
Preparation	1 Access a site with sound clips for download. Here are some copyright free sites: www.findsounds.com, www.freesound.org, www.grsites.com/sounds.

You can use the search box, type a word, such as "cow", "clock ticking" or "motorbike", and then browse the prompted results. Click on the play button to hear the sounds. Right-click on the play button of the sound clip of your choice and select "save target as". Then download the clip. Download about 10 sound clips sharing a common thread that could be included in a narrative.

For example, for Beginner to Elementary levels you may try typing words on findsounds that bear an association with daily routine: "alarm clock", "yawn", "footsteps", "shower", "brushing teeth", "walking downstairs", "teapot", "munching", "slurp", "car starting", "traffic".

At a Pre-intermediate to Intermediate levels you may try typing these words on findsounds for a bank hold-up story: "police siren", "gunshot", "traffic", "scream", "car engine revving", "elevator", "footsteps", "tires screech", "alarm siren", "evil laugh". For a spooky story try: "ghost", "evil laugh", "chain rattling", "creaking door", "crickets", "church bell", "moan", "footsteps", "thunder", "scream".

Alternatively, you may also use sound clips provided by most IWB companion softwares. Simply drag the desired clips from the sound bank to a page.

2 Place the selected sound clips on a page from your companion software.

in class

1 Tell the class that today they are going to listen to some sound clips and, in groups, they are going to write a short story based on what they hear, incorporating those sounds to their story.

2 Reveal the type of story you would like them to write in connection with the sounds. In this instance we will choose a ghost story. Invite the students to anticipate what kinds of sounds they are most likely going to hear (e.g dragging feet, screams, bats flapping their wings). If, at the suggested language level, they don't know some of the words in English, they can say them in L1 and you can write them in English on the board for them. Each time a word for a sound is suggested by a student

2.24 Sound clips

encounter the rest of the class to make that sound. Say one more time, *I couldn't hear a thing* to build up excitement.

3   Ask students to work in groups of four to five. Play, one at a time, all the sound clips from the board. The students must listen and remember them. Now, in their groups, they write a story of about 100 words incorporating at least five of the sounds. They must also decide, as they write the story, where those sounds go in their story. Circulate to provide help.

4   Tell the class that two students from each group will be coming, in turns, to the front. One student will read the group story and the other one will click on the audio icons at the relevant times to provide background sound to the story.

Variation 1

For a more challenging task, choose random sound clips with no apparent connection and ask the students to write creative stories with them.

Variation 2

Instead of downloading and embedding the sound clips, open ten tabs on your Web browser and run a search for a different sound on each tab. Then simply move from tab to tab and click on the sound icons. It is recommended that you look for the sounds about five minutes before the students get to class or while they are engaged in a writing or reading task. Alternatively, you can ask an early finisher to do this for you while you supervise the rest of the students.

Variation 3

Click on the first sound icon and start telling a story. Then ask a student to come to the front to click on a different icon and invite a second volunteer student to continue the story in a logical way incorporating this new sound. Follow the same procedure for the remaining sounds.

Follow-up

Now invite students to write their own stories individually. Share the Internet links with them. They can use a presentation tool of their choice (e.g. Powerpoint/ Keynote/ Voicethread/ Prezi/ Emaze) and write the story in ten slides while placing a different sound clip in each slide. They can email you the document, save it in a pen drive or store it online on Dropbox or Google Drive to share their work in class the following day.

Speaking exchange

Focus	Speaking and Listening practice
Level	Intermediate to Advanced
Time	20–25 minutes for steps 1–6 and 15–20 minutes for step 7
ICT Skills	Online video conferencing tools
Preparation	1 Get in touch with a class of students whose native language is English and who are learning your students' native language. The further resources section in this book offers useful information on finding other classes internationally. Obviously the proposed activity will be more feasible if your students' native language is a world prominent language (e.g. Spanish).
	2 Before the video conference with your partner class takes place, hold a video conference with the partner teacher. That way you can test the video conferencing tool and, most importantly, establish a game plan. You may use Skype or an online video conferencing tool such as www.aol.com/av, www.sifonr.com or www.meetings.io. In this case the teachers decide to have a speaking activity around the theme of animals in zoos and choose the same four questions for the students to have discussions in groups. The questions for your class would be in English and the questions for the partner class would be the same ones but in their L2, that is, your students' L1.

in class

1 Tell the class that today they are going to have a videoconference with another group of students in another country whose mother tongue is English and who are studying your students' L1.

2 Explain that each class will be engaged in a speaking activity with the same speaking questions in L2 before the videoconference takes place. Then they will go online and exchange thoughts in L1.

3 Ask the students to work in groups of four to six and ask them to think of two words for animals that the rest of the students should know and two "difficult" words for animals for the language level. The students, in their groups, challenge each other. They can say the word for the animals in L1 for the other people in the group to say in English. At an intermediate level the "easy" words could be *tiger* and *parrot* and the "difficult" ones *skunk* and *squirrel.*

4 Now write on the board, or dictate, the conversation questions that you chose for this speaking exchange. e.g.

- Do you like zoos?

- Do zoos serve a purpose?

- Do you think that the animals in zoos are happy?

- What are the good things and bad things of zoos?

Speaking exchange

5   Let the students discuss these questions in groups. Circulate to provide help and make vocabulary suggestions. Write relevant vocabulary on the board.

6   In plenary mode, invite a few students to share out their answers with the rest of the class. Draw attention to the notes on the board for good word combinations, accurate pronunciation and correct use of grammar.

7   Open the video conferencing tool and start the speaking exchange with the partner class. The students this time will answer the questions in their own L1. For instance, if you are teaching a class of students whose first language is Spanish, that is the language that your students will be using. This provides each group of students tailor-made exposure to authentic listening from native speakers. In addition, their minds will be preconditioned as they will have already been engaged in conversational exchanges around the topic and related vocabulary. Take good note of useful words and expressions used in English by the partner class. You may allow each class seven to ten minutes to answer the whole list of questions and encourage participation or you may choose one question and ask students from both classes to answer that question in both languages, then move on to the next question and so on.

Variation 1

Use a sound recording tool, such as Pamela or Audacity, for a voice recording of the partner class. Then upload the file online to an online storage site such as Dropbox or Google Drive or to a class blog or wiki if you have one for your students to listen to it outside class hours. You may also devise a listening comprehension activity with questions about the content of the recording.

Variation 2

In addition to agreeing on a topic for conversation and a list of topic-related questions, it is also a good idea to anticipate a list of useful words and expressions that the partner students will most likely be using in the video conference. The teachers can explore that vocabulary with the students prior to the speaking activity so that they can use it in the speaking activity itself in L2 (steps 1-6) and later on this will hopefully help them to identify it in the video conference with the partner classroom. This will provide more word exposure and consolidation.

Follow-up

Ask the students to write a summary of what has been shared in the conversation exchange. This could be done with pen and paper or digitally and then posted on a wiki or a blog. You will have to agree on the length of this summary and let the students know that it might be a good idea to take some notes first of the main ideas and then reformulate them in their own words.

The friendliest voice

Focus Listening practice: Raising awareness of features of pronunciation; Analysing spoken discourses

Level All

Time 30–40 minutes

ICT Skills Finding video clips online

Preparation 1 Find video interviews on YouTube of celebrities who are non-native speakers of English and who speak it at different levels of competency. Your students will know most, or at least some, of these popular figures in sports and arts.

Carla Bruni, Penélope Cruz, Roger Federer, Shakira, Cristiano Ronaldo, Laura Pausini, Jürgen Klinsmann, Rafael Nadal, Zhang Ziyi, Gerard Depardieu

You can access YouTube and then type "Carla Bruni interview" (or the name of the person of your choice followed by the word "interview"). You may also decide to exclusively look for videos of people from your students' country. Browse a few videos and choose one with good sound quality.

2 Choose about five videos from different people. You may download them to play them offline in class or copy and paste the links on a Word document or on an email to yourself that you can open in class.

in class

1 Ask your students for famous people from their country that have appeared on TV programmes or on the Internet being interviewed in English (e.g Antonio Banderas, Pau Gasol, Penélope Cruz, Javier Bardem, Esperanza Aguirre, Rafael Nadal, Elsa Pataky, etc.). How do they rate their English? Who is the best speaker of English? Do they know if their English was good five or ten years ago? Is it common for them to speak English?

2 Explain now that you have selected five video clips of people that they probably know who are non-native speakers of English. They are being interviewed in English. Announce the names. Do they know them? What are they famous for?

3 Ask the students to get a piece of paper and write *the friendliest voice* on it. They will be watching five different extracts from these people speaking in English and they will have to decide who, in their view, has the friendliest voice. Write two more criteria on the board, for instance *the sexiest voice* and *the deepest voice*. Now give students three or four minutes to, in pairs, think and write more criteria.

4 Elicit answers and write those criteria the students thought of on the board (ten is a good number). If there aren't enough,

add some yourself (e.g. *the most interesting voice, the most boring voice, the most irritating voice, the easiest to understand, the most difficult to understand, the speaker with the most confidence, the best English, the worst English, the one who speaks the fastest, the one who speaks the slowest,* etc.). Agree on about ten criteria for your students to write on their papers.

5   Now play about forty seconds from each video clip for your students to make decisions for the different criteria.

6   Now ask the students to share their views. Encourage participation.

7   Invite the class to choose one video clip that you can play for a longer time (about two to three minutes). Ask questions about the video to check understanding. You can also write these questions on the board:

   - Did you detect any grammar or pronunciation mistakes?

   - What was particularly good about his/her English?

   - What needs improvement?

Variation 1

You may also choose native voices of English (in this case, skip the questions on step 7 above). This activity, however, works better in my experience with non-native voices as it promotes more critical thinking and seems to arouse more interest.

Variation 2

Do not reveal the names of the people that you selected. When you play the videos, tell your students not to look at the board. You may also turn the projector off momentarily or, better still, hold down the Fn key of your computer and press F5 (or the appropriate function key at the top of the keyboard) to change the projection mode to computer screen only. Ask the students to guess the names of the speakers.

Follow-up

Ask the students to choose one of the videos played in class and give you a written summary of it.

Invite your students to look for well-known native speakers of English speaking other languages. Particularly impressive are the cases of Bradley Cooper and Jodie Foster as speakers of French or Gwyneth Paltrow as speaker of Spanish. They can look for "celebrities who speak other languages" on YouTube or you can also provide these shortened links for YouTube: "celebrities and language learning" (http://bit.ly/o7yiNF), "bilingual celebrities" (http://bit.ly/YKD2PQ).

2.27 Translation exchange

Focus	Written translation
Level	Intermediate
Time	35–45 minutes
ICT Skills	Using online video conferencing tools
Preparation	1 Get in touch with a class of students whose native language is English and who are learning your students' native language. The further resources section in this book offers useful information on finding other classes internationally. Obviously the proposed activity will be more feasible if your students' native language is a world prominent language (e.g. Spanish).

2 Before the video conference with your partner class takes place agree with the participating teacher on a series of sentences that contain key words and phrases around a given topic for the students to translate. In our case we have chosen "travelling by plane" as a topic pitched at an Intermediate level. Both groups should have the same sentences. Ten sentences is a good number. Half of them will be in English and the remaining half in the language that the partner students are learning. Type these sentences on Powerpoint/a word processor/an IWB companion software. These are some sample sentences:

a *The plane is taking off at eight o'clock.*

b *I got stopped going through security.*

c *It was such a long journey!*

d *Would you like a window or an aisle seat?*

e *The cabin bag weight limit is 10 kilos.*

f *Ha de presentarse en el mostrador de facturación con al menos dos horas de antelación.*

g *Me temo que llevo exceso de equipaje.*

h *Todavía no he hecho las maletas.*

i *Si reservas el vuelo en línea es más barato.*

j *El localizador es SL43339.*

3 Agree on a day and time to meet online.

in class

1 Ask the students to get into pairs and give them a couple of minutes to write up a list of things that may bear an association with travelling by plane. It could be single or words or whole phrases and expressions (e.g *airport, flying, airline, check in, turbulence, a smooth flight, flight attendant, going on holiday*).

2   Elicit answers from the students and write interesting vocabulary on the board. Acknowledge all the answers but only make a note of the least obvious (however relevant) words and expressions. For instance, from the example above you would skip *going on holiday* or *airport* but you could write *turbulence* or *a smooth flight*. Ask the students to explain, in English, what those words and expressions mean.

3   Invite the students to create conversation questions with the brainstormed vocabulary (e.g. *Have you ever experienced serious turbulence on a flight?*, *Do you think flying has got better or worse over the years? Why?*, *Which airlines do/don't you like and why?*). Have conversations around the generated questions in plenary mode.

4   Now open the document with the sentences. Ask the students to work individually and to translate them from L1 to L2 or L2 to L1 as applicable.

5   Go online at the agreed time for the students to exchange translations. They can read their translations and place their pieces of paper in front of the camera and/or (if the online tool allows text chat as well) type the sentences in the text box. Translating from L2 to L1 is an easier task and those translations (a–e in the examples above for your class and f–j for the partner class) will most likely be more fluent and accurate. This way the students can draw comparisons and get input, corrections and feedback from native speakers.

6   Finally allow some time for the students to be engaged in conversations around the questions generated in step 3.

Variation 1

The same activity can be conducted by means of creating a private chatroom for both classrooms (e.g.TodaysMeet) and, instead of using voice, typing the translations in it. Alternatively, online blackboards (e.g. TypeWith, Twiddla or PiratePad) are also appropriate platforms.

Variation 2

Instead of made-up sentences, you and your partner teacher may choose a short written news article (or an extract of a longer article). You should look for the same story covered by different newspapers in the two target languages for the students to translate from L1 to L2 and then compare.

Follow-up

Assign a few more sentences as homework and create a private chatroom or an online blackboard. Provide the link for the students to type their sentences there.

2.28

True/False

Focus	Listening practice
Level	All
Time	15–25 minutes
ICT Skills	Playing videos
Preparation	Find a video of about one to three minutes of length that you would like to play in class and which is appropriate for your students' language level. The useful resources section lists various websites containing interesting videos for the language classroom.

in class

1   Tell the class to listen to you carefully for the next couple of minutes. You are going to tell them about the things you did yesterday. Based on the information they get from you they should write down five True/False statements.

2   Talk for about two minutes and tell your students how your day went yesterday. The students listen, take notes and write down those statements.

3   Ask students to work in pairs and exchange statements. They will have to decide which ones are true and which ones are false.

4   Invite several students to read one statement for the rest of the class to decide if it is true or not.

5   Now tell your class that they are going to be engaged in the same kind of activity. This time the listening source will be the video you selected. Play the video twice. Follow the steps above.

6   Play the video a third time to check understanding.

Variation 1

> To speed things up and make it easier, provide three True/False statements yourself and ask the students to add two more. This will be more suitable for lower level classes.

Variation 2

> You can adapt this activity for written texts as well.

Follow-up

> If the video is available online, ask the students to provide a full written transcript of the first minute. They can play the video at home and pause it and rewind it as many times as needed. Provide the transcript next day in class through printed copies or by simply displaying it on the board.

Video board game

Focus	Listening practice
Level	Advanced
Time	20–40 minutes depending on number of videos
ICT Skills	Using online noticeboards/mindmapping tools; isolating fragments from YouTube videos using online tools

Preparation

1. Find 12–15 short video clips on YouTube with interviews. You can type "interview with" followed by a singer/actor/politician's name. You don't have to watch the videos in their entirety; focus on a timeframe of about ten seconds with interesting information or vocabulary in use that is challenging (but not impossible to understand for your students) and choose those fragments for your class.

2. Open an online noticeboard/mindmapping tool. Here are some:

   - www.padlet.com (no registration required). This is my recommended tool for this activity as still video frames from the videos will be displayed on the board (as opposed to links) and, when clicked on them, a large window within the board will open with the video.

   - www.linoit.com
   - www.popplet.com

3. Access an online tool that allows you to select fragments from YouTube videos. Here are some:

   - www.tubechop.com (recommended site)
   - www.splitcd.com (similar to to Tubechop)
   - www.youtubetime.com (this site will only let you choose the start time)

4. Now select the ten-second fragment for your first video by copying and pasting the YouTube URL for that video onto the Tubechop search box. Then choose a start and a finish time for that video (01:23 to 01:33 for instance). Click on "update" and then click on "chop it". Now copy and paste this new URL onto your noticeboard on Padlet. Repeat this procedure with the remaining videos. Drag your videos on your noticeboard and arrange them as desired.

5. Take good note of the generated URL for your noticeboard.

in class

1. Tell your students to work in groups of four or five.

2. Type the URL for your noticeboard on your Web browser and explain to your students that this board contains fragments of video interviews of about ten seconds each. When you click on one they should listen and write down a transcript of what they hear. At first they can work individually and then confer and write down, as a group, a final version. They should hand you this piece of paper with the group transcript. Click on one video to model the activity and play it twice or three times. Give the students two or three minutes to work on the transcript. Then collect one piece

of paper with the final transcript from each group. Have a look at them and decide which group/s got the closest. Award points (0= blank piece of paper; 1=nice attempt; 2=close enough; 3=good; 4=excellent; 5=perfect). The scores you give cannot be contested.

3   Make sure everyone has understood the procedure and rules of the game that you are about to start. Then click on a second video and follow the same procedure as above. Repeat this with the remaining videos.

4   Once the students have handed you the pieces of paper you may want to replay the video and write on the board any troublesome words or challenging extracts.

Variation 1

For a shorter activity, simply play three or four videos and save the rest for another time. This is suitable for the final stages of a lesson or for times when you are too busy or unable to plan your lessons.

Variation 2

The proposed target language level is Advanced but this can be adapted to all levels depending on the difficulty of the selected fragments. For lower language levels try typing "esl videos" on YouTube and then browse the videos.

Variation 3

I have found that this activity works really well with song snippets as well. You can also look for news broadcasts or documentaries as your video source.

Follow-up

Show the students how to use online noticeboards/mindmapping tools (or have a student demonstrate). Create one and invite them to make short personal presentations on video and then upload the resulting files onto it.

Copy and paste the link from Youtube onto Tubechop. Chop it and copy and paste the new link for the chopped video.

2.30 Voice artists

Focus	Pronunciation: Making voice recordings from transcripts
Level	Beginner to Intermediate
Time	20–25 minutes
ICT Skills	Using screen recorder tools
Preparation	Find video footage from your current textbook. Ideally, the accompanying DVD or digital book should have the option of activating subtitles. Videos that exploit functional language for situations (e.g. shopping, asking for directions, ordering food, checking in at hotels, asking for and offering help) are ideal for this activity.

in class

1   Play the video and do activities related to it as suggested by the teacher's book or photocopy worksheets that may go hand in hand with the video. Alternatively devise your own activities and exploitation of the video material.

2   Activate the subtitles for the video if you have that option. Otherwise distribute copies of the transcript for the video. Set up groups in class. Each group should have as many students as the number of characters that can be found in the video (usually two or three for these types of videos).

3   Tell the groups that each student in the group will take the part of one of the characters in the video.

4   Play the video. Silence the sound and activate the subtitles. The students, in their groups, look at the screen and read out the subtitles when it's their turn.

5   Invite one group to come up to the front to do step 4 for the whole class. This time, just before you play the video, open the screen recorder tool and make a screen recording of the video footage accompanied by the students' voices. As an alternative, you can use online screen recorders, such as Screencast-O-Matic.

Variation 1

Instead of working with videos from your textbook series, find suitable videos with subtitles on the Internet. The video series *The Flatmates* is highly recommendable for Elementary to Intermediate levels (look for *The Flatmates* play list on the BBC Learning English Channel on YouTube). For Upper-intermediate and Advanced levels you may use extracts from films on DVD.

Variation 2

This variation focuses more on writing rather than on listening. Choose an extract from a film featuring people having a conversation. Alternatively run a search on YouTube for "best/ famous movie quotes/scenes/dialogues". Play the short extract/s with no sound and ask the students to provide transcripts.

Voice artists

Make screen recordings with the students' voices and then compare with the real dialogues.

Follow-up

Ask the students to try this at home using online screen recorder tools such as Screencast-O-Matic. Then access those videos online and play a few in class.

Ask a couple of students to record a short video with a mobile phone featuring a dialogue. Then upload the video to the computer and ask two different students to do the dubbing.

Set up a dubbing competition. Then the resulting video clips can be uploaded to a school website or class blog for the students to vote on their favourite ones.

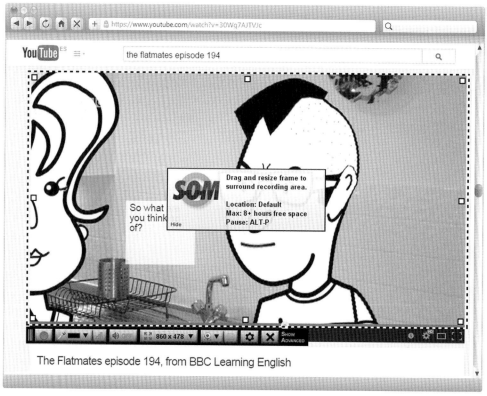

Using Screencast-O-Matic

CHAPTER 4
4.3 TEXT-BASED ACTIVITIES

3.1 A moment in time

Focus	Recalling written texts; conversation around written texts
Level	All
Time	20–30 minutes
ICT Skills	Creating word clouds with online applications
Preparation	1 From a graded reader that your students have just read or are about to finish reading, select three pages that contain key moments in the story. Select within those pages 10–15 key words from each page.
	2 Now access a free word cloud generator on the Internet (see word cloud generators). Create three different word clouds each containing the selected words from one page. If possible, take a screenshot of each word cloud and paste them onto three slides of the presentation tool of your choice (e.g. Powerpoint/ Keynote/ Voicethread/ Prezi/ Emaze) or three pages from your IWB companion software in no particular order. Alternatively, save the links for each of the word clouds so that they can be opened in class.

in class

1 Show the first word cloud on the screen. Ask your students if they can guess what the source for those words is. If no one can tell you, give them a clue such as *it's something you have read (or are reading) for this class.*

Word cloud for Operation Osprey (David Hill, Helbling Languages)

2 Ask the students to work in groups of four or five. Can they guess the moment in time in the story by looking at the words displayed on the screen? Give the groups a couple of minutes and then elicit answers from the class.

3.1 A moment in time

3   Now tell the groups that you will be showing two more pages with, again, key words from different moments in the story. Ask them to take pen and paper to take down a few questions that you are about to dictate:

- *What happened immediately after?*

- *What happened immediately before?*

- *Why did he/she/they...?*

- *If you were to include five more key words to this page, which words would they be?*

If you are doing this activity with an Elementary–Pre-intermediate class, it is best to dictate these questions in L1.

4   Show the second word cloud and keep it on the board for two or three minutes. Encourage the students to discuss the questions in their groups and create their own questions for *why did he/ she/they...?* regarding the motives of the main characters for their courses of action. Repeat this for the last page, and then ask students if they can arrange the word clouds sequentially.

5   In plenary mode review the word clouds and encourage the groups to share their answers.

Variation 1

This activity can also be done by simply typing the words on Powerpoint slides or pages from your IWB companion software. The word clouds, however, will generate more excitement in the classroom.

Variation 2

If your students do not have an assigned graded reader, you can also choose three or four reading passages from your textbook that the students have already read. Create a word cloud for each of the selected texts and encourage the students to try to recall the texts from the key content words. This is also a good opportunity to recycle lexis.

Follow-up

Show the students how to use Wordle or the word cloud generator of your choice. You can also provide a few links for video tutorials that can be found on the Internet. Ask the students to choose another page from the book and create a word cloud with 10-15 key words from it. Then open three or four word clouds in class to have conversations around them.

3.2 Actions and locations

Focus	Grammar: Present continuous
Level	Beginner to Elementary
Time	10–15 minutes
ICT Skills	Typing text; using a dice tool; hiding text (optional)
Preparation	1 Make a list of 11 verbs used in the present continuous that are appropriate for the suggested language level. Complete the sentences in a logical way. Here are some possible examples:

- I am having my hair cut   *at the hairdressers.*
- I am dancing disco music   *at the disco.*
- I am sunbathing   *on the beach.*
- I am studying   *at the library.*
- I am walking the dog   *at the park.*
- I am waiting for the bus   *at the bus stop.*
- I am eating lunch   *at the dining table.*
- I am opening the umbrella   *under the rain.*
- I am cooking lunch   *in the kitchen.*
- I am driving my car   *on the road.*
- I am riding a bicycle   *up a mountain.*

2 Open a blank page from the companion software and type each half of each of the sentences as individual items. Drag all the movable pieces of text from the first half of the sentences to the left in no particular order. Drag all the movable pieces of text from the second half of the sentences to the right in no particular order. Now number each piece of text, starting with number 2 (you can use the pen tool for this). Your page might look like this:

2 I am having my hair cut	2 *at the bus stop.*
3 I am dancing disco music	3 *on the road.*
4 I am sunbathing	4 *at the disco.*
5 I am studying	5 *on the beach.*
6 I am walking the dog	6 *at the hairdressers.*
7 I am waiting for the bus	7 *under the rain.*
8 I am eating lunch	8 *at the park.*
9 I am opening the umbrella	9 *up a mountain.*
10 I am cooking lunch	10 *at the dining table.*
11 I am driving my car	11 *at the library.*
12 I am riding a bicycle	12 *in the kitchen.*

3.2 Actions and locations

in class

1   Show the page with the typed sentences in halves and ask the students to work in groups of three. Explain that the groups, in turns, will come up to the board and mime two halves for the other students to guess, e.g. *I am riding a bicycle at the dining table.*

2   Open the dice tool and select to roll two dice. If you don't have this tool or you don't want to use it, get two real dice. Now explain that the students in the front will have to roll the two dice twice. The combined numbers will assign them a piece of text, first from the left and second from the right. In our example above the dice showed a total of 12 the first time they were rolled and a total of 10 for the second time.

3   Now invite the first group to come up to the front. If you are using the dice tool from the companion software, ask the rest of the students not to look at the board until the students in the front have rolled their dice and closed the dice tool.

4   Next the students from the group in the front should mime as a team the generated sentence for the rest of the class to guess the action and location. Some combinations will be more hilarious, and more difficult to perform and guess, than others.

5   Invite all the groups to come to the front and, in turns, mime the generated actions and locations.

Variation 1

Instead of using real or virtual dice you can create two solid rectangles, place them on the top layer, drag one of them to the bottom left corner and the other one to the bottom right corner, lock both rectangles and then drag the typed phrases behind them. Then the students in the front will drag one typed phrase from each of the rectangles and immediately bring them back behind while the rest of the students look away.

Variation 2

Ask the students to write similar actions and locations on pieces of paper. Collect the pieces of paper and type or write the most interesting ones on the page. Replace some of the texts and let the students be involved in some more miming and guessing.

Follow-up

Ask volunteer students to take pictures of usual actions in unusual locations. For example they could take a picture of themselves while they are holding an umbrella in their bathroom at home. Encourage them to get creative and to also produce pictures in good taste. Then they can store the pictures in pen drives and share them in class the following day.

3.3 Bilingual blog

Focus	Writing: Blog entries
Level	All
Time	10–15 minutes for Day 1; 20–25 minutes for Day 2; 10–15 minutes for Day 3
ICT Skills	Setting up a blog; adding your students to the blog as editors
Preparation	

1 Get in touch with a class of students whose native language is English and who are learning your students' native language within the first two months of the school year. The further resources section in this book offers useful information on finding other classes internationally.
In ideal circumstances both classes of students should be studying the language at the same level but this is not essential.

2 Agree with the collaborating teacher to create a blog for both classes of students. See Chapter 3, 3.3 blogs and wikis for information on free blogging sites. For this activity I suggest creating a blog on Wordpress where both teachers are administrators. Then negotiate about six to 12 topics that will be covered by both classes to be included in the blog. Assuming that both classes of students are at an Intermediate language level these are some possible topics: health, the environment, friends, technology, the arts, crime, travel, fashion, food, education and work. Create a different page for each topic and choose a template for the blog. Depending on the template chosen the blog will feature a menu on the side or on the top with the different sections.

3 Invite the students to join the blog and grant them rights as editors. That way they will be allowed to publish and to edit other users' posts.

in class

Day 1

1 Open the blog in class and show the students the different sections. There is no content at the moment but they will eventually be incorporating content through their collaborations. Explain that you have established a partnership with another group of students who are studying their L1. The idea behind this bilingual blog is that both groups of students write in L2 to practise writing. As every participating student will be granted rights of editor, they will be able to correct mistakes and polish the style of posts written by the partner students. Your students must promise to:

- write regularly in English in the relevant sections
- make any necessary corrections to posts written in your student's L1.

2 Collect valid email addresses from your students so that you can invite them to join the blog as editors.

3.3 Bilingual blog

Day 2

1 Do conversation practice around one of the topics included in the blog. You may prepare a set of questions or use relevant material from your textbook. Suggest useful vocabulary and expressions as your students are engaged in conversations.

2 Give the students around ten minutes to write, on paper, about what they have just discussed orally. They may focus on one conversation question in particular or give a general written account of the speaking session. Stress the importance of using some of the vocabulary and expressions that you have written on the board. If there are Internet connected devices in the class, they may access the blog and type in class. Otherwise, they will have to type their written texts into the blog when they get home (or at a computer lab or library or with a laptop or tablet). They need to make sure that once they log in they select the corresponding page for the topic they are writing about. You may also create subpages within pages so that each section on your blog features its own menu. In that case they would select the corresponding subpage.

Day 3

1 Access the page for the blog where your students typed their texts. Praise the students for participating and highlight good use of words and expressions and underline possible mistakes. Have the texts already been edited by the students from the partner class? Focus attention to those changes. If some corrections have been made, invite the students to read the comments again outside class hours.

2 Check whether the partner students have already written entries in any of the blog sections. If they have, ask your students to make any necessary corrections outside class hours.

3 It's a good idea to allot ten minutes for writing practice in class once or twice a week. My suggestion is to do this immediately after a speaking session, as the students can reflect on a given subject and can incorporate their classmates' ideas and feedback as well as useful vocabulary that you have introduced. Language acquisition and retention are most fruitful when we ask our students to do things with the language in different ways, including writing. In my experience writing in class is the most neglected skill. This type of activity provides regular writing practice for the students with minimal intervention from you, thus saving you time correcting students' work. It is also important that you spend some time revisiting the edited texts in class on the interactive whiteboard/screen for consolidation.

3.3 Bilingual blog

Variation 1

The main aim of the activity is to provide writing practice. You can also ask both classes of students to write in L1 from time to time as well. That way all the students get to read texts written by native speakers.

Variation 2

Obviously a blog can contain much more than text material. You may also invite the students to post pictures or videos related to the topics included in the blog.

Variation 3

If you are teaching a Beginner to Elementary class, you may approach Intermediate to Advanced students in your school who may be willing to edit your students blog entries. These students could be given extra credit or this could be part of community service that is required by certain institutions for graduation.

Follow-up

In addition to writing in L2 and peer-editing the students may also have private text or video chats or the teachers may arrange a few class videoconference sessions during the school year.

Bilingual blog. Notice the topics in the menu

3.4 British English or American English?

Focus	Vocabulary: British English and American English
Level	Intermediate
Time	15–20 minutes
ICT Skills	Typing text, dragging objects, board annotations
Preparation	1 Find word lists that include British English terms and their American English counterparts online. This can be easily done by googling: "American English versus British English words". Choose about 18–20 in total. Alternatively, choose items from the suggested sets here.

American English	British English
candy (sweets)	bill (check)
trashcan (dustbin)	flat (apartment)
parking lot (car park)	trainers (sneakers)
cookie (biscuit)	trousers (pants)
soccer (football)	taxi (cab)
closet (wardrobe)	autumn (fall)
pharmacy (chemist's)	petrol (gas)
French fries (chips)	film (movie)

2   If you are using the words above, type, one by one, the words that are not in brackets. Drag them around the screen in no particular order. Make a written or mental note of the words in brackets.

in class

1   Show students the document you have created. Tell them that what they can see on the board is a selection of words from two varieties of English: British and American.

2   The students get a piece of paper and draw two columns long and wide enough to fit the words. In our case, eight words per column. They should head the columns "American English" and "British English". Now they have a few minutes to copy the words from the board that they know in the correct columns.

3   The students compare notes and make any necessary corrections.

4   Drag all the words to the bottom of the screen and draw one vertical line in the middle of the screen. Write "British English" up on the left hand side. Write "American English" up on the right hand side. Invite the students to come up to the board and drag the words to the correct columns, leaving enough space to the right of each word to write a new word.

5   Confirm with your students that the words have been placed correctly. Now ask the students if they know the counterparts

for the two varieties of English (i.e. the words in brackets above). Elicit answers. Write the words (or ask students to come up to the board to do it). Help with any words whose pronunciation may be troublesome at that language level (for instance, *wardrobe, chemist's* or *biscuit*).

6   Finally, ask the students to work in pairs. Student A looks up to the board and student B looks away or closes her eyes. Student A calls out any five or six typed or written words for his partner to say the American or British counterpart. Then they switch roles.

7   Additionally, you may find two short video clips or listening passages from your textbook or from the Internet that are good examples of the two varieties of English. Play the extracts and ask the students for any peculiar features of pronunciation that they may notice.

Variation 1

At a Pre-intermediate level, choose 8–10 words from one variety and type those words and their counterparts, thus having a total of 16–20 words. If you are using the words above, choose either the 16 words from the left column or the 16 words from the right column. Type them one by one and place them on the screen in no particular order. The students then match the words they see.

Variation 2

Instead of using the companion software, use the online word cloud generator Wordle and do steps 1 and 2 from the main activity.

Follow-up

Ask the students to write about 5–10 lines trying to incorporate as many of the American English words as they can. These two titles will work well for the suggested words: *At the movies* or *Hanging out*.

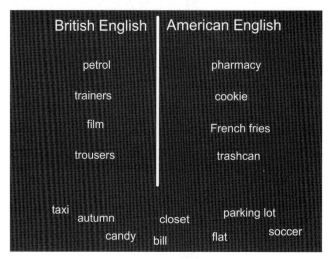

Dragging the words to the right columns

3.5 Categories

Focus	Vocabulary review
Level	Pre-intermediate to Advanced
Time	10–20 minutes
ICT Skills	Browsing the Web
Preparation	This activity makes use of the free online game Scattergories, which can be accessed from any of any of these links:

- http://www.hasbro.com/games/swf/scattergories_demo3.swf (shortened link: http://bit.ly/YE1sS)

- http://www.mp3rocket.me/games/73_36083/Scattergories/Scattergories.htm (shortened link: http://bit.ly/17kaRqg)

Players have to throw a die with the letters of the alphabet. Depending on what letter the die shows, they have to think of words starting with that letter for the various categories listed on the screen within a given time. Access the online game to get familiar with it before you introduce it to the students in class. For detailed instructions: http://en.wikipedia.org/wiki/Scattergories.

in class

1 Ask the students to work in groups of four or five and give them about five minutes to compile a list of board games that they know. If there are students who are not familiar with the term *board game*, run a search for images on Google and show the prompted images on the board.

2 Elicit names for games from your class. Do you have any of these games at home? Do you have a digital version of the game such as a copy on CD, an app on your phone/tablet or software installed in your computer? Can you play any of these games online? What are the aims? What's your favorite?

3 Access the online game Scattergories. Ask a student to explain how the game is played. In the unlikely case that no one knows, explain yourself. Tell the groups that they need one piece of paper per group where they will be numbering the twelve different categories displayed on the screen (they do not need to copy the categories).

4 Click on the die to determine the letter to be used and then click on the timer. When the time is up, elicit answers from the groups and award them points. You may need to collect the papers from the groups and read the answers yourself to avoid potential cheating.

Variation 1

Some of the categories, such as US State Capitals or stones and gems, will be very challenging for the students. You can simply skip those and reduce the number of categories, to 10 or even five.

3.5 Categories

Variation 2

Access the game before you see your class. Click on the die and the timer and wait for the computer answers to show on the screen. Then take a screenshot of the answers and copy and paste it onto a blank page. Use the pen tool to place a blotch of ink over the answers, revealing only the first two letters of each answer. Repeat this three or four more times, placing each screenshot on a different page. Ask the students to guess what the hidden words are. In this instance, they will not need to write down the answers. Any player from any group can call them out. Gradually erase the digital ink covering the words to make it easier. Stay alert for the students' answers.

Variation 3

Access the game before you see the class. As in Variation 2, play the game yourself and copy down the answers on a piece of paper. Once in class, with the students sitting in groups, say: *fruit or vegetable starting with P.* Then start calling out the remaining letters, leaving a few seconds in between letters (P-E-A-C-H). Any student can call out the word at any time. When a student from a group makes a correct guess, move on to the next word (thing that you wear: P-Y-J-A-M-A-S, etc.).

Follow-up

Give the link to your students and encourage them to play the game at home.

Scattergories

3.6 Delving deeper

Focus	Vocabulary: High frequency word combinations (noun+noun / verb+noun)
Level	Pre-intermediate to Intermediate
Time	8–10 minutes per word
ICT Skills	Browsing the Web
Preparation	1 Select two or three highly frequent nouns which your students know at this language level (e.g. *taxi, table, light, friend*).

2 Access the online concordancer just-the-word (www.just-the-word. com). Alternatively you can also use these sites for this activity:

- www.netspeak.org

- www.lextutor.ca/concordancers/concord_e.html

- http://nav.stringnet.org/

3 Run a search for the target words (e.g. *taxi*) and notice high frequency combinations (*taxi*+noun and verb+*taxi*).

in class

1 Access the Wikipedia entry for *taxi* and ask the students to take a look at the first three lines of the article (you may need to enlarge the view of the webpage). Tell them that you will give them about a minute and then, in pairs, they will have to recall all the words closely related to *taxi* found in this intro for the article.

2 Minimize the Web browser and ask the students to work in pairs and compile a list of related words. Then, in plenary mode, elicit words from the students and write them on the board (*cab, vehicle, hire, driver, passenger, ride, public transport, pick-up, drop-off, share*).

3 Now tell them that you are going to do a bit of research on how the word *taxi* combines with other nouns or verbs. Access just-the-word and direct attention to *taxi*+noun and verb+*taxi* combinations.

- *taxi*+noun: *taxi queue, taxi rank, taxi fare, taxi ride.*

- verb+*taxi*: *get a taxi, take a taxi to, go by taxi, call a taxi, hail a taxi, share a taxi, wait for a taxi*

4 Clarify meanings by asking questions such as *What does to hail a taxi mean?* or *When we hail a taxi, what body gesture do we make?*

5 Ask for a volunteer to come to the front. Ask this student to choose one of these combinations without revealing it and give her two choices. She will have to convey it through either drawing it on the board without using letters or numbers or through mime.

6   Repeat step 5 with a few more students.

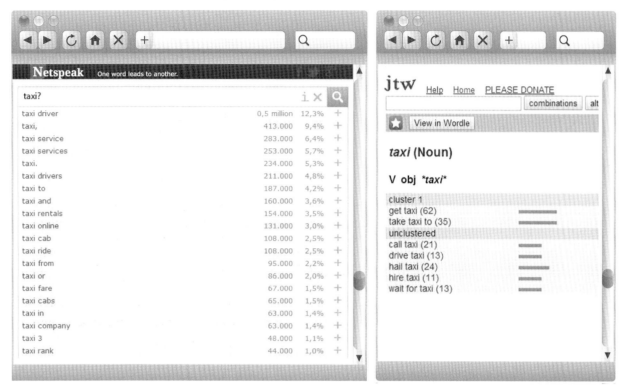

Using lexical tools, Netspeak and Just-the-word, to look for collocations for "taxi"

7   You may want to "delve deeper" into how the next word that you selected for the class combines with other words.

Variation 1

This activity also works well with delexical verbs (*have, take, make, give, go, do*).

Variation 2

Ask the students to write sentences which are true or/and true of themselves using the word combinations (*The last time I shared a taxi was…/I hardly ever take a taxi/The nearest taxi rank from my apartment is…* etc.).

Follow-up

Write about ten high-frequency English words on the board. Ask the students to choose one and, at home, run a search on just-the-word. They should select two word combinations that they find interesting and useful for the class. Then next day, ask the students to work in groups of four to six to share their word combinations and give explanations when necessary.

3.7 Dreams

Focus	Speaking and reading: Interpreting dreams
Level	Intermediate
Time	25–40 minutes
ICT Skills	Browsing the Web
Preparation	1 Access the websites below, which give interpretations of recurring themes for dreams, to make sure they will be active when you do the activity. Select one or two for the activity.

- www.dreammoods.com

- www.dreamdictionary.org

- www.thecuriousdreamer.com

- www.sleeps.com

2 Look in a dictionary or in an online corpus-derived tool (see Chapter 3, 3.6 lexical tools) for different common collocations with the word *dream*. Write them down on a piece of paper. Here are some examples:

have a dream, interpret a dream, remember a dream, awake from a dream, a dream come true, a dream house, a bad dream, my dreams are shattered, not in my wildest dreams, hopes and dreams

in class

1 Write two or three of the expressions above leaving a gapped line for the word dream (e.g. *a ... come true*). Ask your students if they can guess what the missing word is. Elicit other possible word combinations with the target word and provide the rest of the expressions that you wrote down.

2 Ask in class if anyone remembers what they dreamt last night. In case no one does, or no one is willing to share their dream, tell them about something that you dreamt or make it up.

3 Now ask the students to work in groups of four to six and identify common recurring dreams. You may need to give a couple of examples, such as being trapped in an elevator or teeth falling out. Students need to compile a list of a few recurring dreams and have a speaking discussion about what emotions or events might trigger those dreams.

4 In plenary mode invite the groups to share their lists of recurring dreams and their interpretations.

5 Now access the online source/s given at the top and check out a few of the dreams that the students have mentioned and read them aloud while highlighting interesting vocabulary and expressions. Did their interpretations match the ones on the site/s?

3.7 Dreams

Variation 1

Before you see the students copy and paste a few recurring dreams (one per page) together with the interpretations. Use the pen tool to cover the words for the recurring dreams so as not to give them away. Ask the students to read and guess what the dreams are about. Here is one for dreaming about Facebook (the words in italics are the ones you want to cover with blotches of ink).

To dream about *your Facebook page* represents your desires to expand your social circle. You need to reach out to others in a more direct and personal way. It is time to get out there and experience life.

Source: www.dreammoods.com

Variation 2

Before you see the students, copy and paste the same texts from Variation 1. This time, instead of crossing out the words for the recurring dreams, cross out other key words from the interpretations. Here's the same example from above with other words (in italics) hidden from view.

To dream about your Facebook page represents your desires to expand your *social* circle. You need to *reach* out to others in a more direct and personal way. It is time to get out there and experience *life*.

Follow-up

Ask your students to explore more interpretations of recurring dreams at home and start off the class next day with their findings.

3.8 Find someone who

Focus	Vocabulary: Binomials
Level	Advanced
Time	30–50 minutes
ICT Skills	Creating a private chat room; copying and pasting text; onscreen annotations
Preparation	

1   Select about eight binomials (strong collocations made up of two words linked by conjunctions or sometimes prepositions) that you would like your students to practise in class. You can find many lists on the Internet or else you can scan for examples in your current textbook. Here are a few examples: *look and see, the dos and don'ts, peace and quiet, from rags to riches, again and again, bright and early, now and again, high and dry.*

2   Based on the selected binomials, prepare a set of *find someone who...* items for your students. *Find someone who...* is a speaking activity where students are given a checklist with a set of questions and they walk around the classroom engaging in short conversations in order to find classmates who can answer yes to the questions. This activity is good for e.g., contrasting present perfect and past simple (*Have you ever...?/ Yes, I have/When did you...?*), or to practise question formation with modal verbs (*Can you...?*) or with auxiliary verbs in present simple or past simple (*Do you.../Did you...?*). In this case we will turn the activity into a writing activity by using a chatroom allowing private messages as the medium for the written exchanges. Here is a possible list of items for conversation using the binomials above:

Find someone who...

1   ...is going to **look and see** if she can get a job this summer.

2   ... can tell you **the do's and don'ts** of Facebook.

3   ...enjoys the **peace and quiet** of the countryside.

4   ...knows someone who has gone **from rags to riches**.

5   ...keeps making the same mistake **again and again**.

6   ...gets up **bright and early** at weekends.

7   ...goes to the cinema **now and again**.

8   ...has ever been left **high and dry**.

3   Choose a site that provides private chatrooms and allows sending and receiving private messages for the people logged on. Recommended site: Neatchat.com. Alternative sites: Tinychat. com, Chatzy.com

3.8 Find someone who

in class We will contemplate three different scenarios for this activity.

a   A classroom or a language lab with an interactive whiteboard or a computer and a data projector. Each student has an Internet connected device.

b   A classroom or a language lab with an interactive whiteboard or a computer and a data projector. There are enough Internet connected devices for the students to share (a ratio of 1:2 or 1:3).

c   Outside class hours. Each student uses his own Internet connected device. The text from the conversations is copied, pasted and saved. Then it is retrieved in the classroom and displayed in the interactive whiteboard or screen.

1   Write on the board the recommended chat sites listed above. Ask your class if they have ever used them. Open the site of your choice and create a private chat room. Looking at the interface, ask students What kinds of things can the users do in it? (some chat rooms these days allow video chat, uploading files, pictures, print a copy of the texts, etc.).

2   Ask your students to type the generated URL for the private chatroom in their devices and create a nickname. Give them about five minutes to greet each other and chat without revealing their real names. Ask a few questions yourself to break the ice.

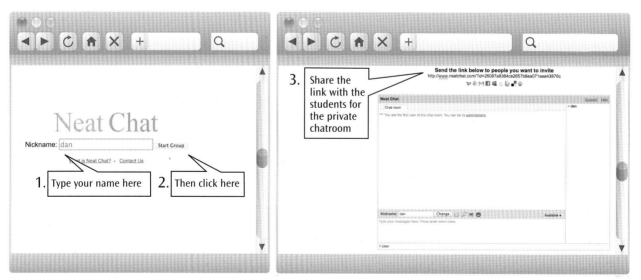

Follow these steps to create a private chat room on Neat Chat

3   Now dictate or type in the chat room the list of *Find someone who...* items and explain the aim of the activity. The students should be sending and receiving private messages within the chat room and having text conversations about the given items (e.g. *Are you going to look and see if you can get a job this summer? – I would love to – Where do you think you could find a job? – Bartending at*

3.8 Find someone who

the weekends, I guess, etc.). When no one is interacting with them, they can always type something in the general chat room. Tell the students not to close the different chat boxes. If you are teaching a large size class, you can have two groups in the chat room.

4   Keep the activity going for about 15 minutes. Now choose a nickname from the list and ask who that student was. Ask a question from the list to see if this student had a conversation about that item. Ask any of the students involved to copy and paste that fragment of their conversation onto the general room. Based on what the students see on their screens or the board, invite the rest of the students to ask questions to have further, spoken, conversations. Underline key words on the board or suggest more accurate vocabulary. Ask students to spot any grammar mistakes.

5   Repeat step 4 with a few more students and have a speaking/text editing session around the items with the binomials.

Variation 1

This activity is adaptable for all levels.

For Elementary to Pre-intermediate levels you may want to try use of present simple (e.g. *find someone who... plays a sport/speaks two or more languages/listens to music everyday/has a big family/cooks well/doesn't like football/thinks girls are better students than boys*).

For Intermediate to Upper-intermediate levels, you may try expressions with *make* and *do* (e.g. *find someone who is planning on doing some shopping this weekend/does exercise regularly/can make a suggestion for this class/usually does the dishes at home/has made a grammar mistake while chatting to you/didn't make his or her bed this morning/didn't do any homework yesterday/can make three wishes*).

Variation 2

I have also found that this activity works really well with selected vocabulary from reading passages as it provides plenty of drilling and exposure to the target words and expressions in a meaningful and enjoyable environment while also providing speaking and writing practice for the students. Here's an example from a reading passage from *For Real Pre-intermediate*, Martyn Hobbs and Julia Starr Keddle, Helbling Languages 2010, page 50.

Find someone who... thinks this class is tough/didn't get enough sleep last night/has been to an awesome place you haven't been to/can tell you the name of a cute celebrity/likes doing his or her own thing/thinks that this class is cool/is hanging out this weekend/is going to have a good night's sleep tonight.

Follow-up

Set up a schedule with days and times for the students to meet online outside class hours and chat.

Googling for numbers

Focus	Numbers (1–10,000); Vocabulary for jobs
Level	Elementary to Pre-intermediate
Time	20–25 minutes
ICT Skills	Browsing the Web
Preparation	None

in class

1   Think about words for jobs that you would like to revise in class. Tell your class what the people who have those jobs typically do without revealing what jobs you have in mind. For instance, *A ... makes sure that his or her students learn* or *A ... looks after patients.*

2   Now ask students to work pairs. Each student must choose five jobs whose names they know in English and generate sentences like the ones above without disclosing the words for the jobs.

3   Elicit a few sentences from various students for the rest of the class to guess the jobs.

4   Now tell the class that you would like to review the numbers. Ask If you were to google the word "secretary", what would the number of search results be? Ask a few students to guess (at the time of writing it was 341 million). Ask the question: *What does a secretary do? (A secretary types letters/writes emails/answers the phone/does paperwork*, etc.). Now choose one of your students' sentences and "google" it using inverted commas. How many times will this appear on the Internet? Ask the students to guess and "google" it (Google listed the search query for "a secretary types letters" 3,080 times).

5   Ask the students to work in groups of four or five. Ask a student to read one of her sentences. Make corrections if necessary. Now the students in their groups and in turns must guess the number of times they think this sentence is listed on Google. Give the groups about a minute for each student within each group to call out a number. Then google the sentence for the students to find out. The student who gets closest to the number of results showing on the screen gets a point.

6   Ask a different student to read out his sentence. Repeat step 5 a few times to keep this activity going for another 10-15 minutes.

Variation 1

The main focus of this activity is revising numbers in a fun and effective way. At the suggested language level you could also combine this revision of numbers with language practice on the present simple and the use of frequency adverbs. In this case you

Googling for numbers

would ask the students to think of verbs for daily routine (e.g. *get up, go to school, go to work, have a drink,*). Then they would produce sentences in the present simple with frequency adverbs (*I usually get up at seven o'clock*). Other possible language areas are: *can*, quantifiers, *there is/there are*, past simple of irregular verbs or comparatives.

Variation 2

Access www.googlefight.com instead of Google. Googlefight is a site that compares search results for two search queries. Enter the two words or phrases in the boxes for the stick figures to fight and render the results. You could ask the students to guess which of the two given jobs/foods/places in town/countries/adjectives for physical description/health problems/animals/weather words, etc. are more popular.

Variation 3

The focus here is not on numbers but on collocations at a very basic level. Ask the students for highly common English nouns that they know (e.g. *telephone, police, computer, house, street*). Which word starting with "a", "b", "c" etc. collocates well after the word *telephone?* Give the students a few minutes to think about it (individually or in small groups) and elicit answers. Then type the word *telephone* followed by space and the letter *a.* The students will be able to identify *telephone area code.* Try out a few other letters of the alphabet (e.g. *telephone book, telephone box, conversation, country codes, codes, directory,…*).

Follow-up

Encourage the students to google phrases with inverted commas when they are not sure that they are writing something accurately. Given two search queries, the one prompting the highest number of results is likely to be the correct choice. This is particularly useful with the use of infinitive or gerund after certain verbs, choice of prepositions after verbs and adjectives or use of *do* and *make* among others.

Search for "a secretary answers the phone": 9180 results

Happiness is...

Focus	Listening practice: Dictation
Level	Intermediate
Time	10–15 minutes
ICT Skills	Typing text; creating objects
Preparation	

1   Find four interesting quotes on happiness on the Internet and write them down on a piece of paper. No quote should be over two lines long. Here are four quotes that you may want to use for the suggested language level.

- *Happiness isn't something ready made. It comes from your own actions.* Dalai Lama.

- *Happiness in intelligent people is the rarest thing I know.* Ernest Hemingway.

- *Count your age by friends, not years. Count your life by smiles, not tears.* John Lennon.

- *Rules for happiness: something to do, someone to love, something to hope for.* Immanuel Kant.

2   Now type these quotes on a page and hide them by crossing them out with the pen tool or by creating solid rectangles and placing them over the typed sentences.

3   Type the names of the four people these quotes are attributed to in any order and place them on the bottom of the screen.

in class

1   Write this on the board: *Happiness is...* Ask your students to complete the sentence. Give them about a minute to do this.

2   Ask the students to read out their sentences. Make comments and encourage comments from their ideas or definitions of happiness.

3   Now tell your class that you are going to read out four definitions of happiness made by famous people. The students need to write them down what you are going to read. Explain to them that you are only going to read the definitions once at normal speed and that they most likely will not manage to take down everything even though the vocabulary is not particularly difficult.

4   Read out at normal speed the four quotes, pausing for about six seconds after each quote.

5   Ask the students to work in groups of four or five, compare what they have written and see if they can, as a group, rewrite the definitions so that they are as close to what you read as possible.

6   Elicit answers from the groups and confirm by unveiling the hidden quotes on the board. Ask them to match the quotes with the names displayed on the bottom.

Happiness is...

Variation 1

Here are some alternative quotes that may be more suitable for Elementary to Pre-intermediate level:

- *Happiness is like a kiss. You must share it to enjoy it.* Bernard Meltzer.

- *Happiness is nothing more than good health and a bad memory.* Albert Schweitzer.

- *You can be happy where you are.* Joel Osteen.

- *Success is getting what you want. Happiness is wanting what you get.* Dale Carnegie.

Variation 2

You can try this activity out just before you are ready to start a new textbook unit on a given topic as a lead-in. For instance, *art is..., money is..., computers are..., English is..., food is..., men are..., women are..., travelling is...* Look for quotes on these topics and follow the steps indicated above.

Follow-up

Ask the students to look for other quotes on that topic on the Internet and ask them to bring them to class next day to be read out and shared.

If you have a blog or wiki for the class, ask the students to type out their definitions of happiness there. Or you can also create a hashtag for Twitter and invite your students to share them out there. Access the blog, wiki or your Twitter account the next day in class and take a look at the generated sentences on the board.

3.11

Health and illness

Focus	Vocabulary for health and illness
Level	Advanced
Time	20–30 minutes
ICT Skills	Typing text
Preparation	

1   Select 15-20 target words and expressions from your textbook around a given topic. In this case, as an example, I have chosen the topic health and illness. Alternatively find useful words and expressions and collocations for this language level on the Internet or from other sources at your disposal. Here are some examples:

a nagging headache, to go into remission, to go down with the flu, blocked up nose, blurred vision, red blotches all over my skin, a runny nose, to pull a muscle, arm in a sling, leg in a plaster cast, to be on the mend, to pick up a stomach bug, my rash hasn't cleared up, to have blisters, to be on crutches, a speedy recovery, to have stitches removed, to have shooting pain, a chipped bone, to be on medication

2   Open your IWB companion software or a presentation tool of your choice (e.g. Powerpoint/ Keynote/ Voicethread/ Prezi/ Emaze) and place each expression on a different page/slide.

in class

1   If the vocabulary that you have selected comes from a handout or the textbook, review it with the students and/or do the proposed activities. Otherwise, you could dictate the expressions. Read out, for instance, *a nagging...* for the students to call out the possible missing word. When a student says *headache*, confirm this is the expression that you selected for them and ask them to write it down. Next read out *to go into rem....* If no one knows, then provide the next syllable or sound or string of sounds for the missing word (as in *to go into remiss...*). You may need to write some of the words on the board. Do not clarify meaning at this stage.

2   Once the students have copied all the expressions, review them again, one by one, and confirm and clarify meaning (e.g. *What does a nagging headache mean? Can you give me a synonym for nagging? To go into remission. Does that sound like the patient is getting better or worse?*).

3   Now open the document that you created. Ask your class if they are familiar with a memory game that is usually played to remember students' names in the first day/s of class. The first student says *my name is...* (followed by her name), then the second student has to say the first person's name and add his name (*her name is Paola, my name is Aldo*), then the third student has to recall the previous students' name and add his name (*her name is Paola, his name is Aldo and my name is Bruno*) and so on.

4   Based on that type of memorization activity, they are going to do something similar with the expressions on the board. The first student will have to construct a logical sentence using the expression displayed on the board, as in *I have a nagging headache* or *This weather is giving me a nagging headache*. Then open the next page (or slide in Powerpoint) for the second student to recall what the first student said and to add something of his own with the expression he can see now (*This weather is giving Anke a nagging headache, My uncle has just gone into remission*). Open the third page for the third student to say *This weather is giving Anke a nagging headache, Dieter's uncle has just gone into remission, Don't come too close to me as I've just gone down with the flu*. Follow this procedure with eight or nine other students.

5   If it gets too difficult at some point, the rest of the class can always help to recall the expressions in order.

6   If you have more students than expressions, you can model the activity with 10–20 students and then ask the students to work in pairs or groups. This requires all the pairs/groups moving at the same pace as you cannot monitor each group. Simply estimate the time the groups need to recall the generated sentences. It is, however, still a very productive way to memorize the expressions.

Note: if you decide to choose words and expressions for health and illness, it is best to avoid words for serious medical conditions, as this might be a compromising issue in some instances.

Variation 1

Provide useful word combinations and collocations on each page for the students to choose from. (e.g. for the first expression type *to have a nagging/splitting/bad/mild/lingering headache*).

Variation 2

In addition to creating full sentences, ask the students to mime the expressions as they are being said and recalled. This will help memorization and retention.

Variation 3

This technique also works well to drill grammar structures at various language levels (e.g. u*sed to/didn't use to*, modal verbs, reported speech, relative clauses.)

Follow-up

Ask your students to write up conversation questions incorporating the lexis drilled in class for a speaking session next time you see them.

3.12 *Luckily/Unluckily*

Focus	Writing: Contrasting statements
Level	Elementary to Pre-intermediate
Time	20–25 minutes
ICT Skills	Typing and dragging objects
Preparation	None

in class

1 Tell the students that you are going to give them two or three minutes to think about and write a couple of good things that happened to them yesterday (or over the weekend if you are seeing them on a Monday) and a couple of not so good things.

2 Invite students to read out their sentences and ask follow-up questions. For instance, if a student says *my favourite football team won*, you can ask questions such as *were they playing home or away?, what was the final score?, are they having a good season?*, etc.

3 Now explain the mechanics of the activity. The students will be working in pairs. Student A should write a sentence starting with the word *luckily*. Then Student B should write another sentence showing contrast and starting with the word *unluckily*. Then Student A writes a new sentence with *luckily* again showing contrast with the preceding sentence and so on. For example:

A: *Luckily, my favourite football team won yesterday.*

B: *Unluckily, the best player got injured.*

A: *Luckily, it wasn't anything serious.*

B: *Unluckily, he will miss out next game.*

A: *Luckily, I don't think he will.*

B: *Unluckily, if he plays, he might get injured again.*

4 Do the first example in plenary mode, typing the generated sentences on the computer. Then jumble up the sentences and ask the students to order them as they were created.

5 Now ask the students to work in pairs, take a piece of paper and cut it up into eight strips. Each student collects four strips to write down on each a "luckily" or "unluckily" sentence. Give enough time for the pairs of students to write their sentences. As they write them, they should place the strips of paper below each other forming logical sequences.

6 Ask the students to swap strips of papers with other pairs and try to place them in logical order. Give them about eight to ten minutes to exchange strips of paper with as many pairs as they can.

3.12 *Luckily/Unluckily*

Variation 1

For time saving purposes, prepare a "luckily/unluckily" story beforehand to model the activity. Type each sentence independently and then jumble them up on the screen. Open the document in class and ask the students to place the sentences in order. Then do steps 5 and 6 from the main activity.

Variation 2

You can recycle these sentences to practise concessive clauses with *although, though, even though* (e.g. *Even though my favourite football team won yesterday, the best player got injured.*)

Follow-up

Ask the students to produce their own *luckily/unluckily* sentences, jumble them up and share them online for the other students to place in order. They may use Padlet or Popplet or Linoit as Web 2.0 tools.

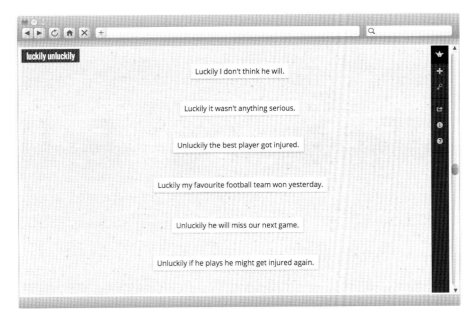

Sentence strips on Padlet for students to drag and sequence in order

3.13

Make or *do?*

Focus	Delexical verbs: Expressions with *make* and *do*
Level	Pre-intermediate to Intermediate
Time	30–40 minutes
ICT Skills	Typing text
Preparation	1 Make a list of common expressions with *make* and *do* that you would like to introduce or review in class with your students.

2 Type each expression on a different page in no particular order.

3 Open another page. Type or write the questions on the left and the responses on the right

   - *Can I just ask you something?*   - *Sure.*
   - *Sorry to bother you.*   - *Go ahead*

4 Write each expression on a card or strip of paper. Write on the back of each card a translation into the students' first language, e.g. *do a favour* on the front and *hacer un favor* on the back. Here's a list of 16 expressions for the suggested language level.

   do a favour, do a good job, do an exam, do sport, do homework, do research, do the shopping, do your best,

   make a mistake make the bed, make a complaint, make a good/ bad decision, make an effort, make a mess, make a noise, make a suggestion

in class

1 Write on the board: *Excuse me.* Ask the students in which situations they might hear or use themselves this (e.g. to ask for permission, to ask someone politely to move so that you can walk past, to tell someone you are leaving a place, just before showing disagreement, to call someone's attention just before you ask them a question). Draw attention to the last usage. Can they think of any alternative expressions?

2 Tell the students that they are going to do work on expressions with *make* and *do*. Elicit expressions from the students.

3 Give each student a card/piece of paper with an expression. Explain that everyone will have to stand up, walk around the classroom, meet another classmate and replicate the following conversation exchange

   - Student A (has a card with do a favour): *Sorry to bother you/Can I just ask you something?*

   - Student B: *Sure/Go ahead.*

   - Student A: *Do you happen to know/Do you know/Can you tell me what "hacer un favor" is in English?*

- Student B: *It's do a favour. Now do you happen to know/do you know/can you tell me what "cometer un error" is in English?* (Student B's card reads *make a mistake* on the front).

Student A: *That's make a mistake.*

Then those students exchange cards and find other speaking partners and replicate the conversation exchange with the new cards.

4   Give students about eight to ten minutes to have as many conversations as they can with as many different classmates as possible. They must exchange cards each time.

5   Now show the document created with the expressions. Open the first page. Ask the students to think of a question that includes that expression. For example, if the expression is *do a favour,* they may say *When is the last time you did someone a favour?* With *make a mistake,* they may ask *What is a common mistake you make when you speak English?* Some of the expressions, such as *do sport,* are more likely to generate more questions and discussion than others (*Do you do sport? What sports do you do? Do you like doing sport? How often/When do you do sport?*). Let the students have short conversations around the generated question/s. Follow this procedure with the remaining pages.

Variation 1

If step 5 is time-consuming, you may decide to focus only on five to eight expressions that are likely to generate conversation.

Variation 2

You may also block from view the verbs *make* and *do* so that each expression is displayed without the verb. Then ask the students to call out the missing verb on each page.

Variation 3

This technique of producing bilingual cards and displaying a record of the target language on the board can be applied to just about anything you might want to introduce or revise.

Follow-up

Once used, do not get rid of the cards. Label each card (or most of them) by writing a tag name (in this case "make and do") on a corner. Keep the cards together with a rubber band. Then do the same with the next set of expressions (expressions with *get,* telling the time, prepositions of place, etc.). Have as many groups of students as vocabulary sets and ask the students to work in groups and test each other. Then the groups can swap stacks of cards several times.

3.14 Mistake detectives

Focus	Grammar and Vocabulary: Correcting errors
Level	Pre-intermediate to Intermediate
Time	15–20 minutes
ICT Skills	Annotating words on the board
Preparation	None

in class

1 Select some conversation questions from the textbook, a handout, the Internet, create your own or ask the students to create relevant conversation questions around target vocabulary. These are good sources for conversation questions from the Internet:

- http://iteslj.org/questions/

- http://esldiscussions.com/

- www.eslconversationquestions.com/

- www.englishcurrent.com/esl-conversation-questions-discussion/

- http://teflpedia.com/Category:Conversation_questions

As suggested above, you may pick some conversation questions from the sources above and provide key words for the students to write the questions. For these questions provide the prompts below.

- *What are the pros and cons of living in a city? - pros/cons/city*

- *What differences do you think there are between life in a city and in the country? - differences/city/country*

- *Where do you think it's best to grow up? - where/good/grow up*

- *Would you prefer to live in an old city with a lot of history, or a more modern one? - prefer/old city/history/modern city*

(source: teflpedia.com)

2 Assign some time for the students to work in groups of three to six and discuss the questions.

3 Circulate to provide help. Each time you detect a lexical or grammatical error, write down on a piece of paper the actual words uttered by the student. When you have three or four, walk to the front of the classroom and copy your notes on the board. Open a different page for each note. Limit the number of notes to ten. Write just recurrent mistakes and do not reveal which student/s made those mistakes to prevent demotivation.

4 In plenary mode, have a few students answer the questions.

5   Now tell the students to get some paper. You will be showing them, one at a time, errors that you detected while they were engaged in conversations in their groups. Show the first page with the first error and ask the students to rewrite on paper what's on the board and try to fix the error. Stay on that page for about 30–40 seconds and move to the next page with a new error. Again, ask the students to fix the error. Repeat this procedure with the remaining pages.

6   Go back to the first page and, in plenary mode, ask the students how they edited what you wrote on it. Repeat this with the remaining pages.

Variation 1

If you want to make things easier for the students, underline the problem areas. In some cases there may not be errors as such but perhaps there's room for better word accuracy. Underline the word/s you would like them to replace.

Variation 2

Write on two or three pages utterances with no mistakes. Ask the students to decide what's wrong and what's correct.

Variation/Follow-up

Do not do corrections in class. Instead of writing the errors, open a word processing document and type the errors as they are being generated. Then print copies (or make this document available on the Internet through Google Docs or by emailing it to the students) and ask the students to correct the mistakes for homework.

3.15 Newsflash

Focus	Recalling written texts through writing; Text editing
Level	Intermediate to Advanced
Time	20–25 minutes
ICT Skills	Typing text; copying and pasting text
Preparation	Choose a news article of interest for your class from an online English newspaper of about 200-400 words. Break it down into portions. Copy and paste each portion (about 100-150 words) on a different page of a document from your companion software or slide in the presentation tool of your choice (e.g. Powerpoint/ Keynote/ Voicethread/ Prezi/ Emaze) After a page or slide with written text, leave a blank page or slide. Depending on the length of the article your final document will be have two to four pages/slides of written text and an equal number of blank pages/slides.

in class

1   Ask the class about today's news. What's in the news today? Have they watched any news reports on television or the Internet? Have they read any newspapers?

2   Go online and access an online newspaper with news in English. Some newspapers nowadays have English versions. For instance if you are based in Spain you may want to access the English version of El País or if you are in Italy you may want to access La Stampa in English. By doing so the students will be more familiar with the stories on the front pages as some of them will feature local or national news of interest. This will prompt more participation. Discuss with your students some of the articles. Draw attention to the headlines and make sure your students understand what is conveyed by them. Encourage speaking by inviting the students to tell the stories they are familiar with in their own words.

3   Now ask the students to work in groups of four or five. Tell them that you are going to display a news article for them on the board. The article is divided into two to four parts and you will only leave each portion for about 30 seconds, just enough time for them to read quickly and take a few notes. Then they will see a blank page for about ten seconds (this will give them time to finish writing notes), then another page showing the next bit of the article and so on. It is their task to get a piece of paper and take as many notes as they can and also to try to memorize as much as possible so that they can reconstruct the original text as closely as possible in their groups.

4   Open the document and stay on the first page for about 30 seconds, then show a blank page for about ten seconds, move on to the next page with written text and display it for 30 seconds and so on. The students at this stage work individually.

5   The students can now confer and compare their notes and write down

3.15 Newsflash

the news story. Reassure them that their shared piece of writing does not have to match the length of the original but they should rather focus on content. For an article of 400 words, a reconstructed text of about 100 words is fine.

6   The groups read out their texts in turns.

7   Display the article one more time and highlight key words from it. Clarify understanding.

Variation 1

Copy and paste each portion of text twice on different pages. Using the pen tool, cover every other word with a blotch of ink. This time, instead of having to recall the text in writing, the students will have to recall the missing words orally.

Variation 2

Instead of looking for a news article, select a reading passage from your textbook. You can recycle a text that has already been seen in class recently or you can choose a text that you are about to use.

Variation 3

An interesting alternative to the one suggested above is to lead in to the main activity by showing news on video. A highly recommended source for the suggested language level is One-minute World news from the BBC site (www.bbc.co.uk).

Follow-up

Ask the students to find a newspaper story they are interested in or a reading passage from the textbook and underline about ten key content words from it. Next they underline the two words that come immediately both before and after each underlined word. Then they copy down the resulting chunks on a piece of paper. Invite them to recall the sentences where those words are found through writing or speaking.

One-minute World News from the BBC

3.16 Present perfect and past simple

Focus	Grammar: Present perfect and past simple; Speaking practice
Level	Elementary to Intermediate
Time	25–35 minutes
ICT Skills	Typing text
Preparation	Open your IWB software or presentation tool of your choice (e.g. Powerpoint/ Keynote/ Voicethread/ Prezi/ Emaze)and type on a page about eight to ten interesting sentences about yourself incorporating the use of present perfect and the past simple. Some sentences will be true and some will be not. Type them out in any order, e.g.

- I've written four books.

- I've visited 20 countries.

- I lived in the USA for four years.

- I met Bill Clinton in 2001.

- I've never tried skiing.

- I once saw a UFO.

- I studied Arabic for two years.

- I started learning English when I was 18.

- I've been a teacher for 21 years.

  not true at the time of writing:

- I've visited 20 countries (I believe it's 19).

- I once saw a UFO (I imagined I did when I was a child).

- I studied Arabic for two years (It was for one year; not two).

in class

1   Review with your class the use of the past simple (finished past actions when the time is mentioned or understood) and the present perfect (past actions when the time is not mentioned/ recent past actions/unfinished actions).

2   Write on the board:

I lived/I have lived   I visited/I have visited   I was/I have been

Give the students a couple of minutes to write down two or three sentences that are true of themselves using any of the verb forms above (e.g. *I have lived in Astorga all my life/I visited the Pompidou Center last time I was in Paris/I have been to Paris three times*).

3   Elicit a few sentences from the students, check their accuracy and elaborate on whether the students who have called out sentences have used those tenses correctly or not.

3.16 Present perfect and past simple

4   Now display on the board the document that you created. Tell your students that most of those sentences reveal true things about yourself. Which ones do they think they are? Invite the students to ask you as many questions as they can in light of those questions (e.g. *When did you live in the USA?/What were you doing there?/Did you enjoy the experience?/What did you like the best?*).

5   Now ask the students to work in groups of three. Give them about five minutes to write about five to ten sentences about themselves using the past simple and the present perfect. They may incorporate the sentences they have already written. Most sentences should be true and some not. Circulate while they are writing their sentences to provide help and check accuracy.

6   The students, in their groups and in turns, read out their sentences for the groups to decide if they think they are true or not. It is also essential that, as in step 4, questions are asked and additional details are given in answer to those questions.

7   Invite various students to read out their sentences and share them with the whole class in addition to providing extra information.

Variation 1

This activity also works well for these grammar points at a Beginner to Elementary level: present simple, frequency adverbs, *can* for ability, *like/enjoy/dislike*.

Variation 2

Use the power of images for a more time-consuming activity in terms of preparation but one that is perhaps both more memorable and more enjoyable. Look for images that can illustrate your sentences (for the first sentence a typewriter or a computer and an image of a book or four images of books; for the second one a world map with a red tick over 20 different countries, etc.). Ask the students to guess the sentences first, and then confirm what the sentences are.

Follow-up

If you have a wiki or a class blog invite the students to write again the sentences about themselves without revealing their names. Open the wiki or blog in class next day for the class to guess who is who. This also provides good feedback as any possible mistakes can be pointed out and corrected. It is true that blogs and wikis are not tools primarily used for grammar practice but in this instance they allow shared viewing in class and peer editing outside class time. If you do not have these collaborative platforms, this can also be easily done by setting up a chat room on the spot in Todaysmeet and sharing the URL with the class.

3.17 Rhyming dictionaries

Focus	Pronunciation: Vowels
Level	Elementary to Intermediate
Time	10–15 minutes
ICT Skills	Browsing the Web
Preparation	

1   Select a vowel sound for your students to work on in class. Your textbook may include a phonemic chart with the sounds of English and word examples. You may want to select pronunciation exercises within the textbook units. You can also find various phonemic charts on the Internet. Here we will be focusing on /iː/. Choose words from your textbook or make a list of your own examples including a variety of common spellings for this sound. Here are some examples: *heat, sea, police, machine, field, dream, sleep, leave, seen.*

2   Go online and become familiar with rhyming dictionaries. There are many to choose from. Here are some examples:

- www.rhymebrain.com (strongly recommended because it is very visually appealing for an interactive whiteboard or a large screen for the class).

- www.rhymezone.com

- www.rhymer.com

- www.poetryforkids.com

- www.wikirhymer.com

- www.rhymebox.com

in class

1   Write /iː/ on the board. Ask your class for examples of English words that contain that vowel sound and write them on the board. Correct pronunciation when necessary.

2   Give the students a couple of minutes to write sentences including as many of the words written on the board as they can.

3   Invite the students to read out their sentences.

4   Now divide your students into two large groups. It is not essential that they sit together. They may remain in their seats but each student must know the group he/she is in. Write on the board one of the words that you selected for the activity and invite any student to call out a word that rhymes with it. In the meantime, access a rhyming dictionary but hide it from view by turning the projector off momentarily or, better still, by holding down the Fn key of your computer and pressing F5 (or the appropriate function key at the top of the keyboard) to change the projection mode to computer screen only. Check with the rhyming dictionary for the accurate answers given by the students and give the teams points.

3.17 Rhyming dictionaries

5   In some instances it will be difficult for the students to think of rhyming words. When that happens, start spelling out a word that they probably know from the ones listed in the dictionary and stay alert for the first student to call it out.

6   After each round you may want to change the projection mode to both computer and screen for the students to see the words displayed on the screen. Then you can highlight the pronunciation of relevant words for the language level that your students may not have been aware of.

Variation 1

Look for the selected words beforehand and take some screenshots of the rhyming words. Then copy and paste the resulting images on a word processing programme or presentation tool of your choice (e.g. Powerpoint/ Keynote/ Voicethread/ Prezi/ Emaze) or on an IWB companion software programme. Open the document in class, showing and hiding the screenshots as appropriate.

Variation 2

Get into the habit of always having a rhyming dictionary available by accessing it from your Web browser. Minimize the browser. If you want to illustrate a given pronunciation or correct a mispronounced word, simply maximize the browser, type the word in the text box and exemplify the pronunciation with the rhyming words.

Variation 3

If there are enough Internet connected devices in the classroom, give the students the selected words and the links for the dictionaries and invite them to write short poems or rap songs featuring rhyming words.

Follow-up

Building on Variation 3, ask the students to improve their poems or songs at home and either post them on a blog or wiki or read them out in class next day.

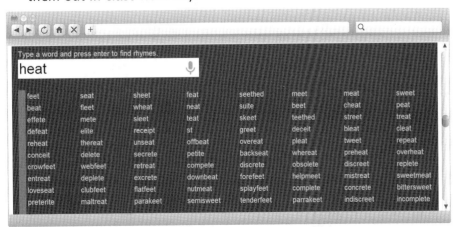

Rhyming words for "heat" on Rhymebrain

3.18

Right a wrong

Focus Grammar and Vocabulary: Correcting errors

Level Intermediate to Advanced

Time Chat session: 15–20 minutes. Vocabulary/grammar corrections: 10–15 minutes

ICT Skills Copying and pasting text or screen capture tool; creating a private chat room online; pen tool

Preparation Set up a private chat room for your students to have online text-based conversations. These are some possible sites for this activity:

- www.neatchat.com,

- www.tinychat.com,

- www.todaysmeet.com,

- www.voxli.com,

- www.chatzy.com.

If there are enough Internet connected devices in the classroom, you may hold this chat session in class. You may also take the students to a computer lab or library with enough Internet-connected computers. Otherwise you can agree on a day and time and a length of time to meet online outside school hours.

in class

1 Make sure that students can access the chat room that you have created for the chat session if they are chatting from school. Have some students help out peers if necessary. If you are having the chat session outside school hours, greet students as they join in.

2 Have the chat session. This could be a general natural conversation or you may decide to talk around a specific topic, e.g. movies, sports, a graded reader the students are reading at the moment, what everybody did at the weekend, what everybody will be doing at the weekend, etc. Join in as moderator and encourage participation.

3 Once the given time for the chat session has expired, retrieve the whole text or portions of it by copying and pasting it onto a Word document or by taking snapshots and displaying the written extracts on a page from the companion software.

4 Use the pen tool or highlighter to draw attention to grammatical mistakes or inaccurate use of lexical items and also to emphasize example of good use of English.

5 Ask the students to work in pairs and discuss what might be wrong about those things that have just been highlighted and what changes, if any, they would make.

6 After a few minutes invite the students to share their thoughts on the matter and provide your feedback as well.

3.18 Right a wrong

Variation 1

Alternatively you may print paper copies of the conversation (or relevant extracts).

Variation 2

Do not highlight anything from the retrieved text/s and let the students decide what is in need of correction and what other changes they would make.

Variation 3

Do not highlight anything from the retrieved text/s and let the students highlight examples of good use of English.

Follow-up

If you do this kind of activity a few times during the school year, keep a log of the most common or important errors from each session that have already been corrected in class, type them on a document, make copies and ask the students to correct them at home.

3.19 Sound it

Focus	Vocabulary for sounds
Level	Upper-intermediate to Advanced
Time	20–30 minutes
ICT Skills	Writing on the board
Preparation	Look for about 15–20 words related to sounds that people, animals or things make that you would like to review or introduce for the suggested language level. Here are some examples for you to choose from:

grunt, whistle, belch, hiccup, sneeze, yell, snore, slurp, giggle, stammer, whisper, boo, gasp, sigh, mumble, creak, sizzle, crunch, whoosh, screech, rattle, bang, splash, tap, drip, slam, purr, chirp, bark, roar, squeak, croak, grunt, hum, howl, buzz

in class

Note: If the students have Internet access in class or if they have enough monolingual paper dictionaries, do step 3 in class. Otherwise, it can be done at home.

1 Tell the students to close their eyes for about a minute and to listen attentively for any sounds they may perceive. During that time, you might want to produce a few sounds yourself. For instance, you can drag a chair or a table, crumple a piece of paper, clear your throat or blow your nose.

2 The students can now open their eyes. Elicit answers. In addition to the noises that you may have made, the students should also share any other sounds that they may have heard, such as noise from passing traffic, someone coughing, the hum of the data projector, etc. Help with vocabulary when necessary.

3 Assign each student one of the selected words. If necessary some of the students can be assigned the same words. Each student should look their word up in a dictionary. They need to write the word on one side of an index card or piece of paper and the definition on the other together with at least one example of that word in use, replacing the word in question by a dotted line, as shown here:

Front of the card	Back of the card
mumble	To speak quietly and in a way that is not clear so that the words are difficult to understand. She … something about being too busy. "I'm sorry," he …

(definition and examples from www.cambridge.dictionary.org)

3.19 Sound it

4   Collect all the cards from the students. Ask students to work in groups of five or six. Distribute all the cards, giving each group of students any five or six cards face down. Students make a stack of cards face down, have a look at the first one and try to call out the missing word. They follow the same procedure with the rest. When they have used all the cards, they should exchange cards with another group. Encourage groups to exchange cards as many times as they wish. Even if they get same sets of cards twice or three times, explain that this lexical exposure is beneficial.

5   Open a blank page. Now ask the students that if they had to choose three particularly difficult words from the 15-20, which ones would they be? Elicit one word from ten different students. Write each word on a different page, thus having a document displaying ten different words on ten different pages (one word per page). Write the words big and clear.

6   Go to the first page of the document. Tell the students to imagine that they are watching television and that they are flicking through channels. When they see the word displayed on the board, they have to pretend that they have just stumbled upon a programme where they can "hear" that sound. At that point any student can volunteer and provide the background information by explaining what's happening for about 20 or 30 seconds. Immediately after that all the students in the class will have to "produce" that sound.

For instance, the first page shows the word *stammer*. Aleksandra volunteers: *Watching TVP1 now. It's a soap opera. Here's a close-up of a man and woman, who seem to be a couple. Both of them look rather serious. Suddenly the man, clearing his throat, stammers these words: "S-sorry, I d-don't love you any m-more".* *The woman bursts into tears.* At this point the rest of the students will have to stammer *S-sorry, I d-don't love you any m-more* a couple of times.

Now advance to the second page. Let us imagine that the word written on it is *screech*. This time Maciej takes the initiative and says: *This is TVP2 now. This is an action movie. A wrecked police car is chasing some bank robbers on the run. All of a sudden, the car driven by the robbers screeches to a halt. You can see the smoke rising from the wheels.* The students now imitate the sound of screeching tires.

Follow the same procedure with the remaining pages.

Sound it

Variation 1

As an extension of this work, collect all the cards from the students. Open the camera tool from your computer if you have a webcam or an inbuilt camera and place the back of a card in front of the camera lens. Ask the students to work in pairs and look at the board and write down on a piece of paper the missing word. Give them about ten seconds and then flip over the chart to show the word (or say the word aloud). Do the same for the remaining cards.

Variation 2

Again, as an extension of the work provided by this activity, access the website www.wordnik.com and type in, one at a time, the target words, stopping to look at the definitions, tweets with the words, pictures and sounds.

Follow-up

Ask the students to record sounds with their mobile phones. It's not essential that every student makes recordings. They can record sounds in the street or at home. Then the students work in groups of five or six and play the recordings for the group members to say what kind of sound or noise it is in English. Circulate to provide help.

Shuffled letters

Focus	Vocabulary review
Level	All
Time	10–15 minutes
ICT Skills	Typing, infinite cloner (in Notebook for Smart boards) or drag a copy (in Activinspire for Promethean boards)
Preparation	Type all the letters of the alphabet separately and place them at the bottom of a page. Right-click on each one and activate the infinite cloner (in Notebook for Smart boards) or drag a copy (in Activinspire for Promethean boards) feature from the pull-down menu.

in class

1 At the beginning of the lesson ask the students to choose two or three words or expressions that they have recently seen in class.

2 Open the file with the typed letters and ask the students to come up to the board in turn and drag the letters from the selected words to the middle of the screen in any given order and in this way challenge their classmates to call out the words.

Variation 1

Save the last 5–10 minutes of a lesson for the students to select two or three words or expressions that they have seen that day.

Variation 2

Ask a student to come up to the front and drag any seven letters to the middle of the screen (including at least a couple of vowels). Then ask the whole class to write down as many words as they can containing those letters. For an extra challenge limit the search to words related to a certain semantic field.

Variation 3

Ask the students to come up to the front and drag every other letter of the word they have in mind in the correct order. For example, if the word in question is *outstanding*, the board would show o_t_t_n_i_g (or _u_s_a_d_n_). If the class is having trouble guessing the word, an extra letter or two can be added.

Follow-up

Ask the students to create posters with the words and expressions used in this activity at home. They can use technology for this (such as the word cloud generator Wordle) or paper and markers. Decorate the classroom with the posters. Alternatively, open the in-built camera tool of your computer or the webcam and place the posters, one at a time, in front of the camera so that they can be seen enlarged on the board. Ask the students to generate sentences with these words and expressions.

3.21 Teleprompter

Focus	Reading aloud
Level	Pre-intermediate to Intermediate
Time	10–20 minutes
ICT Skills	Copying and pasting text; browsing the Web
Preparation	1 Browse a few online teleprompters – sometimes referred to as autocues. Here are some examples for you to explore:

        - www.cueprompter.com

        - www.easyprompter.com

        - www.onlineteleprompter.com

    2 Now look for a news story of interest to your class. There are many sources for news on the Internet (the reference section lists some). In this case I recommend selecting a news story from www.breakingnewsenglish.com for the suggested language level. Copy and paste the story onto a word processing document. Alternatively, take some text from a reading passage from your digital textbook if possible.

in class

1 Open the document with the news story or reading passage. Ask a student to read the first two sentences and, without announcing it, time him doing so. Tell this student how long it took him to read the sentences. Now ask another student if she can beat that. It is also important that she reads the sentences accurately. Ask a third student to read even faster.

2 Ask the class if they know what a teleprompter, or autocue, is. If anyone knows, let him explain. In any case, go online and look for an image which will show what it is.

3 Copy and paste the text from the document onto the text box for the teleprompter and ask the whole class to choral read the news story aloud with you while trying to keep the same pace. Your text may exceed the maximum number of words to be pasted on the teleprompter. If so, just use the portion of text that the telemprompter will allow you to work with.

4 Try step 3 once more. This time increase the speed to provide an extra challenge.

5 Ask the students if they want to be challenged a third time. Warn them that you will be increasing the speed considerably.

6 Although the main focus is practising reading aloud, you may also want to discuss the news story with the students and have a look at interesting or troublesome vocabulary.

3.21 Teleprompter

Variation 1

Ask the students to write a news story or a personal narrative outside class hours and save the texts in pen drives. They can retrieve their texts in class and then copy and paste them onto the text boxes of the online teleprompters and read them out.

Variation 2

If the Internet connection is failing you may simply display the text on the board and, if you have a laser pen, use it to point from a distance at the text lines moving the pen horizontally from left to right as in reading.

Follow-up

Share the links for the online teleprompters and encourage your students to practise reading and gradually increase the speed at home.

Using Easyprompter

3.22 The missing verb

Focus	Grammar: Phrasal verbs
Level	Upper-intermediate to Advanced
Time	30–40 minutes for Day 1 and 15–20 minutes for Day 2
ICT Skills	Browsing the Web; using on-screen annotation tools; screen capture tools (optional)
Preparation	Option A (in class about five minutes before you see your students)

1   Access the online concordancer just-the-word (www.just-the-word.com). Alternatively, the proposed activity can also be done using these online tools:

- www.lextutor.ca/concordancers/concord_e.html

- http://nav.stringnet.org

- http://fraze.it/

2   Run a search for the word *draw* on just-the-word. Then notice the *draw* (V)+Adv combination link on the right side. Click on it. Now click on the "draw up" link. The concordancer will now provide a list of full or partial sentences found on the Internet with this verb+adverb combination.

3   Follow step 2 with the suggested verbs *end, own, run and turn* followed by the adverb *up*. Access just-the-word on a different tab from your Web browser each time. Minimize the Web browser.

Option B (outside class some time before you do the activity)

Run a search for the target word combinations (see above) and take screenshots of the screens displaying the sentences. Then paste the resulting images on an equal number of pages of your IWB companion software. Place a blotch of ink with the pen tool over the target verbs.

in class

Day 1

1   Write these words on the board: *hurry, get, break, give*. Ask the class: *Can you find a common thread for these words?* (They are high frequency phrasal verbs when followed by *up*).

2   Now write these phrasal verbs on the board: *back up, bring up, cheer up, clean up, dress up, eat up, make up, speak up and throw up*. Ask students to work in pairs or threes and discuss the meanings for a couple of minutes. Then, in plenary mode, elicit definitions or explanations from the students.

3   Tell the students that you are going to show them examples of other phrasal verbs which are a bit more challenging. They will see full or partial sentences of verbs, which have been covered in digital ink, followed by *up*. It is their task to guess the verbs from the context clues.

4   If you took screenshots, show the first page. If you are doing this straight from the Internet (Option A in Preparation above), ask the students not to look at the screen for a few seconds. In combination with your IWB companion software or with free online annotation tools (see page 28, Annotation tools), place a blotch of ink over each occurrence of the target verb on your first tab on your browser. Now give the students time to guess what the verb is.

Screen capture of examples of "end up" in context from just-the-word.
Copy and paste it onto IWB software and then use the pen tool to hide the verb.

5   Repeat step 4 with the remaining verbs.

6   Write on the board all the phrasal verbs seen in this teaching session and ask the students to write a short story of about 50–80 words with one of the following titles: A *day on the beach*, A *terrible nightmare*, *School trip.* They should try to incorporate at least three of the phrasal verbs.

7   Show the class how to look for word combinations on just-the-word (or alternative sites). Choose about 20 different phrasal verbs that you would like to review with the class (including the ones seen today). Assign each student a different phrasal verb (if you have more than 20 students, some of the students can share the same phrasal verb). Tell the students to look for examples of those phrasal verbs with the lexical tool they have just been introduced to outside class hours. They will have to either write down about five or six sentences from the displayed examples on a piece of paper and leave a gap for the verb, or copy and paste those sentences onto a word processing programme and then print a copy (they should edit the sentences and leave a gap where the verbs are).

3.22 The missing verb

Day 2

1 Ask students to work in groups of five or six and collect all the pieces of paper (step 7 above). Distribute the pieces of paper among the groups. Ideally there should be five to six pieces of paper per group but even if you end up with two to three pieces of paper per group, the activity is still productive.

2 Tell the students that, in their groups, they will have to work out what the missing verbs are. When they have done so, they need to exchange papers with another group who have finished. Encourage groups to exchange papers as many times as they can. It is important that they do not write on those papers.

3 Collect the pieces of paper, shuffle them and distribute them again among the groups and repeat step 2.

4 In plenary mode, ask the students what the missing verbs were.

Variation 1

Instead of writing short stories incorporating the verbs, the students can improvise dialogues.

Variation 2

Try this activity with adjective + preposition combinations (e.g. *interested in, keen on, afraid of, good at*). Hide the adjectives from view.

Follow-up

The reference section includes information on online concordancers and lexical tools. Encourage the students to try them at home to help them out in their writing assignments or simply for fun.

Trending topics

Focus	Microreading
Level	Beginner
Time	10–20 minutes
ICT Skills	Browsing the Web
Preparation	Make sure you can access Twitter in the classroom with an existing account.

in class

1 Ask the students if they know what *trending topic* means. Where have they seen this term before? (your students' most likely answer will be in Twitter). How does this translate into their L1? Tell them to, in pairs, compile a list of three trending topics; for school; for their town; for their country; for the world.

It is important that they write words that they know. You will not help them with words they do not know at this stage. For instance, at the suggested language level, the students may be able to write these three words for the trending topic "school": *exams, teachers, boring.*

2 Invite your students to read out their lists to the class.

3 Now access Twitter on the computer and notice the "trending topics" section on the left hand side. Click on the link to change country and choose an English-speaking country. Can the students identify any of the trending topics? What are the tweets about? Click on one trending topic. Focus the students' attention on the screen and ask them how many words they can identify and whether they can fully understand any of the tweets. Find below a screenshot of the first seven tweets displayed on the screen at the time of writing.

I find this microreading material ideal for all language levels but especially so for Beginners as you can raise awareness of common abbreviations in text messaging, use of prepositions, common word combinations and use of grammar. It is also very feasible in most instances to generate conversation questions out of this material that can provide plenty of active exposure to vocabulary. Here are some possible conversation questions for this language level with some of the words from the tweets below:

- *When's your birthday?*
- *Is your birthday coming up (anytime) soon?*
- *What are good birthday gifts?*
- *Are gift cards good gifts?*
- *What can you buy to surprise someone on their birthday?*
- *What are you going to get them?*
- *Can you think of timeless gifts?*

3.23 Trending topics

Help them this time with vocabulary for gifts. The greatest pay-off from generating these conversation questions is in the questions rather than in the answers. By answering the questions the students get plenty of exposure to useful language found in the questions and by thinking about what to answer they are consolidating the target words and phrases.

Tweets for trending topic "Father's Day"

Variation 1

Look for words you are teaching, e.g. *gift*, instead of topics.

Variation 2

You can do this search for a trending topic at home and instead of accessing it live in the classroom, copy and paste the tweets that you think are more interesting from a language standpoint and/or more suitable for creating conversation questions.

Variation 3

Focus the class attention on a word that you want to teach, e.g. *gift*, and access the online dictionary Wordnik. In addition to giving definitions and examples for the various entries, this dictionary also provides sounds and pictures for some of these entries and authentic examples from Twitter where the words are used in context.

Follow-up

Ask the students whether they have Twitter accounts. If so, tell them to tweet something using one of the trending topics that they wrote in step 1 of the activity and tag it preceded by # (as in *I don't like exams #exams* or *I don't like #exams*). Then next day look for those hashtags and have the class take a look at the generated tweets. For those students who do not have a Twitter account, they may just simply write their tweets on paper and read them out in class.

3.24

Vague language

Focus	Spoken grammar: Vague language
Level	Upper-intermediate to Advanced
Time	10–15 minutes
ICT Skills	Browsing the Web; taking screenshots (optional)
Preparation	1 Select two or three language chunks that are common examples of vague language used by native and proficient speakers of English. Here are some examples to choose from:

> List completers: *and things like that, or something like that, and that kind/sort of thing, and stuff like that, and things, and stuff, or whatever, or something, and all that, and everything*
>
> Placeholders: *thingy, whatsit, whatsername, thingummyjig*
>
> Generalisers: *sort of, kind of*
>
> Hedging: *I just sort of, I just feel like, I tend to, I'm not too keen on, I'm not very fond of*

2 Go to Twitter and type one of these language chunks with inverted commas. Take note of six or seven tweets that are good examples of use. You can either type them on a slide of a presentation tool or a page of your companion software or take screenshots and copy and paste them. Repeat this for the remaining phrases. You may simply run a live search in class, which only requires thinking about what language chunks you want to have a look at.

in class

1 Write on the board: - ...*promises/ideas/rumours/memory/feeling* Ask the students to think of an adjective that combines well with these nouns meaning imprecise, not clear. If they have trouble with it, give them the first letter: "v". If at this point nobody knows, say it yourself: *vague*. Ask: *What is a vague promise? Can you draw an example from a real life situation? How about vague ideas and rumours? How about a vague memory or a vague feeling?*

2 Now introduce the concept of vague language. Tell them that the casual use of these language chunks in spoken English is a good indicator to gauge fluency in speakers of English. Today you are going to focus on *or whatever* and *and that sort of thing* (or your chosen phrases). Do students use these phrases casually when speaking, texting on the phone or chatting online?

3 Go on Twitter and type "or whatever" (using inverted commas). The actual use rate of "or whatever" is, as I'm typing this, of about 20 new tweets per minute. You can point this out to your class as evidence of how frequent the use of these language chunk is. Bear in mind that you may find offensive language. If you are not teaching adults, it might be a good idea to sieve through tweets before you see your class. These are some unedited tweets for *or whatever*:

3.24 Vague language

Tweets including "and that sort of thing" and "or whatever"

4 Let the students read the tweets and ask if they need help to understand them. Next ask them to write a tweet on paper using the target language chunks.

5 Invite the students to read out their tweets.

Variation 1

This activity centers around evidence of vague language on Twitter but you can also look for any other language chunks to show language in use.

Variation 2

Make a quick search on Twitter when a student asks you for a word in English, or when you are suggesting a better way of expressing a concept or when you stumble upon an interesting expression in a reading passage or listening extract. The students will be exposed to authentic and contextualised usage of those words and expressions.

Follow-up

Encourage your students to use Twitter to find examples of new language chunks to help understanding and retention.

3.25

Wikidictionary

Focus   Vocabulary review

Level   All

Time   10–15 minutes

ICT Skills   Creating a wiki for the class

Preparation

1   Set up a wiki for the class at the beginning of the school year. The reference section contains some information on wikis. My recommended wiki platform for this activity is wikispaces, as educators can get a free update from the basic plan.

2   Choose about 10–15 topics that you will be covering during the school year. The nature and depth of these topics will vary depending on the target language level. Create a page for each of the selected topics and type on each page a couple of interesting words or expressions related to the topic followed by explanations or definitions. For instance, for the topic travel at an Advanced level, type on the corresponding page:

bustling: busy, noisy, full of people (a bustling city)

unspoilt: not changed by tourism (unspoilt beaches/countryside/nature)

in class

1   Let your students know that you have set up a wiki for the class containing 10–15 different pages associated with an equal number of topics they will be seeing during the school year. Ask them to explain what a wiki is. What is the most popular wiki on the Internet?

2   Look for the video "wikis in plain English", which can be found on YouTube or through Google. After you play this short video you may also play it again, silence the sound and ask the students in turns to describe what is happening (you may need to pause the video from time to time to make things easier for the students).

3   Show the wiki that you have created for the class and collect valid email addresses from the students so that they can be added to the wiki. Explain that, once they join it, they should be typing words and expressions that they see in class related to the topics contained in the wiki, as you have just done with the two examples above. This creates a good environment for them to revise vocabulary as well as a good opportunity for you to devise activities for the class. In addition to typed text, they can also add links to interesting articles or videos.

3.25 Wikidictionary

Wikidictionary. Notice the topics in the menu on the right-hand side. Entries for "travel"

4   These are some activities that you can do in class once the students have incorporated a substantial number of word entries:

- In combination with your IWB companion software or with free online annotation tools, such as, bounce or diigo, place a blotch of ink over the entries. Let the students have a look at the definitions/explanations and give them some time to write down on a piece of paper the words that are hidden from view. Then erase the digital ink for them to check.

- Open a page of your wiki, ask students to work in pairs and write a short story or a mini saga incorporating words from that page. Next ask the students to read out their stories.

- Ask students to work in pairs. Student A looks at the board. Student B looks away. Student A reads out definitions from a page for Student B to guess. Then open a new page from the wiki related to a different topic. Students change roles.

- Open the spotlight application of your IWB companion software and hover over the definitions and explanations so that they are partially revealed. Ask the students to guess the words or expressions.

- Do pronunciation practice with difficult words.

- Try other activities suggested in 3.26 Wrapping things up.

Variation 1

Instead of a topic-driven approach, list the words alphabetically. In this case, each page could contain four letters of the alphabet (page 1 A–D, page 2 E–H, and so on).

Variation 2

You may allow early finishers to come to the front of the classroom and add new words to the wiki or edit content.

Follow-up

Ask students to create content for the wiki outside class hours.

Wrapping things up

Focus	Vocabulary review
Level	All
Time	5–10 minutes
ICT Skills	Creating word clouds with online applications
Preparation	None

in class

1   Type, as teaching happens, into a word processing program vocabulary and expressions that crop up in class. In most instances this type of lexis arises from teachers reformulating spoken utterances in the classroom or when students themselves ask for words they fail to remember or they do not know. For practical purposes have a folded sheet of paper in your pocket where it is easier for you to quickly take it out, unfold it and write this vocabulary on the move.

2   In the last 8–10 minutes of your lesson open an online word cloud generator. Give your students two to three minutes to review the new vocabulary that has cropped up in class (words that you have written on the board or you have spelled out for them). This short time should be enough for you to type into a word processing program these words (which you have written on paper). You can also type them out in the text box from your cloud generator. Copying and pasting them from a word processing program has the advantage of being able to make changes to your poster in terms of adding new words, fixing spelling or retrieving them for other potential posters in the future if the document is saved.

3   Create a word cloud and show it on the screen. Spend the last five minutes of your lesson doing vocabulary-related activities with this word poster. This will help your students to consolidate this lexis. These are just a few teaching ideas to go with the word poster:

- Students work in pairs and play Hangman using the words on the poster.

- Students work in pairs. They each choose a word and draw it for their partner to guess (as in the game of Pictionary).

- Ask a student to choose a word from the screen and provide a definition for the rest of the students to guess.

- Use the screen annotation mode of your IWB companion software (or take a screenshot of the poster and then paste it onto a page of the companion software). Select the pen tool and use it to cover each word except for the first two letters. Then point at the various words for the students to recall. Use the eraser tool to erase the blotch of ink covering the words.

- Ask the students to work in pairs and improvise dialogues where they have to somehow fit in two or three of the words they see on the screen. Give them a couple of minutes and then, in plenary mode, choose one or two pairs to share their dialogues with the class.

- Choose a word from the poster but do not reveal it. The students ask you *yes/no* questions until someone guesses it. Then they can do this activity in pairs.

- Choose a word from the poster and provide two definitions or explanations of it; one being accurate and the other one invented. Students decide which one is correct and which one is wrong. Do this again with two or three more words. Now ask for any volunteer students to do this with other remaining words.

- Whisper a word from the poster to four or five different students. Now ask them to call out words springing to mind that bear an association with it. For instance, for the word *toll* they may say *road, cars, pay, tax, booth, credit card, cash, driver*, etc. The rest of the students will have to identify the word that was whispered to these students. Do this with a few more words by whispering them to different students each time.

Variation 1

Write the words on a piece of paper, save it and then create the word cloud at home. Start off your lesson next day reviewing this vocabulary.

Variation 2

Ask for a volunteer to be in charge of writing this vocabulary on a piece of paper. Choose a different student each time.

Follow-up

If you have a class blog, embed the word clouds on it for reference. The students will be able to access them outside class hours and you may also retrieve them and do vocabulary revision in class as desired. If your blog platform or the word cloud generator will not allow embedding, take a screenshot of it and then paste it.

Word cloud on Wordle with selection of words from a teaching session

Further resources

Interactive whiteboards

www.exchange.smarttech.com Collection of activities for SMART Boards.

www.prometheanplanet.com Teaching resources, free webinars and video tutorials for Promethean boards.

http://resourcecenter.hitachi-software.de/ Software downloads and resources for Starboard boards.

www.mimioconnect.com Lesson plans and activities for Mimio users.

www.e-beam.com Software downloads and resources for Ebeam users.

http://open-sankore.org Open source IWB software.

www.itilt.eu iTILT (interactive Technologies in Language Teaching) project. It promotes integration of the interactive whiteboard into communicative teaching approaches. Also find the training manual which focuses both on technical aspects of using IWBs and methodology for language teachers.

www.whiteboardblog.co.uk Educational blog that looks at the use of technology in the classroom (mainly Interactive Whiteboards or resources that work well on them).

www.teachingenglish.org.uk/search/apachesolr_search/IWB Updated by EFL teachers, it hosts teacher forums on many topics including IWB technology, use and professional development. This link directs to a filtered search of forum threads discussing IWBs.

https://sites.google.com/site/whiteboardmaterials/home Collection of IWB resources.

http://www.teachhub.com/free-interactive-whiteboard-resources Whiteboard resources for teachers.

Websites and blogs on Web 2.0 tools

http://edtechtoolbox.blogspot.com E-learning and Web 2.0 tools.

http://cooltoolsforschools.wikispaces.com Collection of Web 2.0 tools.

www.boxoftricks.net The resources link on the menu provides a very comprehensive list of Web tools.

http://blogs.ihes.com/tech-elt Tom Walton's tech ELT blog.

www.educationaltechnologyinelt.blogspot.com Vicky Saumel's blog on tech tools.

http://quickshout.blogspot.com.es Nick Peachey's blog reviewing Web tools.

www.freetech4teachers.com Richard Byrne's site on free technology resources for teachers.

www.teachertrainingvideos.com Russell Stannard's video tutorials on use of Web 2.0 tools.

http://ozgekaraoglu.edublogs.org Ozge Karaoglu's blog on apps and Web tools.

These links include information for institutions interested in language exchanges on the Internet.

- *www.globalschoolnet.org/pr*

- *http://en.community.epals.com/culture_center/default.aspx*

- *https://education.skype.com/*

Further resources

Exploiting images

http://www.theguardian.com/global/ng-interactive/2014/may/29/-sp-the-guardian-app-for-ios-and-android The Guardian Eyewitness app for iOS and Android

http://www.boston.com/bigpicture News stories on high quality photos

http://blogs.reuters.com/fullfocus High quality photos from Reuters news agency.

www.nationalgeographic.com Worth previewing photos in the people and culture and travel sections.

http://takeaphotoand.wordpress.com Ideas for using images in the ELT classroom.

www.youtube.com Pause the video, take a screenshot of the still frame and paste it onto a digital document to show on the board and generate interest and conversation around it.

www.flickr.com/photos/eltpics Photos taken and uploaded by ELT professionals who make them available copyright-free for non-commercial use.

www.pixabay.com Creative commons photos.

www.thenounproject.com Free public domain icons.

http://search.creativecommons.org Provides access to websites with creative commons content.

http://commons.wikimedia.org Very comprehensive database of creative commons media.

(acknowledgements for the first three links to Tom Walton. Sources retrieved from his blog post Great sources of images for class (not Google Images!) *http://blogs.ihes.com/tech-elt/?p=3799*

Exploiting video

www.lyricstraining.com Music video clips with fill in gaps activities.

www.lvlapp.com Similar to lyricstraining but also includes TED talks, movie scenes and documentaries among others.

www.videojug.com "How to" video guides.

www.wonderhowto.com Short "how to" videos arranged by category

www.eslvideo.com Videos and comprehension questions.

www.simpleenglishvideos.com Videos for English language students including transcripts. Click on the text to play any point in the video.

www.ted.com Educative talks from inspirational speakers.

http://film-english.com Kieran Donaghy's site featuring short videos and lesson plans for ELT.

http://viralelt.wordpress.com Ian James' viral videos for ELT.

http://allatc.wordpress.com Steve Muir and Tom Spain's activities for advanced learners.

http://lessonstream.org Jamie Keddie's site with video activities.

www.nicertube.com Removes YouTube distractions. Enter the YouTube link and select a background type.

http://safeshare.tv Alternative site to nicertube.

www.quietube.com Drag the button to the bookmarks bar and then click the button to remove comments and images of other videos on YouTube.

Further resources

Exploiting audio

www.bbc.co.uk/worldservice/learningenglish Listening material from the BBC for language students.

www.elllo.org 1000+ listening comprehension exercises.

www.esl-lab.com Easy, medium and difficult listening activities.

www.listenaminute.com Close to 500 listening activities listed alphabetically.

www.breakingnewsenglish.com Listening lessons arranged into levels based on news.

www.famouspeoplelessons.com Listening activities based on biographies.

www.eslholidaylessons.com Listening lessons based on holidays.

www.eslpod.com Podcasts for learners of English.

www.podcastsinenglish.com Audio and video listening activities arranged into levels.

www.en.wikipedia.org/wiki/Wikipedia Spoken_articles: Selected articles from Wikipedia on audio.

http://iteslj.org/links/ESL/Listening/Podcasts Directory of podcasts.

https://www.youtube.com/audiolibrary Library of tunes for free download to use in projects. Sign in with a Google account.

Exploiting text

www.lextutor.ca Lexical tool including an online concordancer.

www.forbetterenglish.com Very useful tool to search for collocations.

http://corpus.byu.edu/bnc British National Corpus.

http://nav.stringnet.org Useful lexical tool to search for word patterns.

www.classtools.net/SMS Generate fake phone text messages. Useful for learners to create conversations around new lexis. The chats can be saved and embedded into blogs, websites or wikis. QR Codes can also be generated.

www.quozio.com Create visually attractive quotations.

www.phrase.it Upload a photo and add speech bubbles with text to it.

http://idebate.org/debatabase Database of model written debates with for and against arguments on many topics. Worth checking top 100 debates section.

www.quizlet.com Create your own word lists.

www.learnclick.com Create online gap-filling, drag and drop, dropdown and multiple choice exercises.

Teacher's quick-reference guide

This guide will help you select an activity suitable for your class based on the time you have available and the learning level(s) of your students, and other factors such as the content and language focus. To use it, look down the left-hand column under a particular chapter till you come to a time that's suitable for you, and then look across to see the name of the activity spread across the range of levels it's suited to. Then across again to to find the focus and the activity number.

If you prefer to start with the level of your students, find the level on the top line, then go downwards till you find an activity name, and on that same row you will find the time required, the content focus and language focus, and the activity number. Please note that the guidance is very basic; it allows you to see, when you're thinking of running an activity for the first time, how long the activity is likely to take according to the authors' experience.

Lesson time	Beginner	Elementary	Pre-int	Int	Upper-int	Advanced	Focus	Activity number
Section 1 Image-based activities								
5–10	A thousand words is worth a picture						Vocabulary	1.1
10–15	Changes						Describing people, clothes, present continuous	1.2
30–40				Chindogu			Describing objects and what they're used for	1.3
30–45				Conversation board game			Talking about travel; Writing questions	1.4
20–25	Every bedroom tells a story						Things in the house, likes and dislikes	1.5
Day 1 20 / Day 2 10		Five things					Making personal presentations	1.6
Day 1 20–30 / Day 2 1–25		From Italy to Brazil and back again					Writing and speaking about their own countries	1.7
20–30				Games children play			Present continuous; Talking about children's games	1.8
15–20		Guess what just happened					Connectors and sequencers	1.9
15–20	Life's common objects						Vocabulary for common objects	1.10
Day 1 10–15 / Day 2 15–20		Myths and facts					Past simple	1.11
Day 1 5–10 / Day 2 20–30	Our world						Talking and writing about meaningful objects	1.12
25–35		Personal pictures					Talking about personal pictures; Frequency adverbs	1.13
25–30	Personalizing the textbook						Talking about pictures	1.14

Lesson time	Beginner	Elementary	Pre-int	Int	Upper-int	Advanced	Focus	Activity number
30–40				Proverbs			English proverbs	1.15
10–20	Ranking						Vocab for fruit	1.16
5–10	Say it with a painting						Vocab review	1.17
10–20	Speak, spoke, spoken						Past simple and past participle of irregular verbs	1.18
10–15	Spot the difference						Prep of place; there is/are	1.19
15–20		The tallest person in the world					Superlatives	1.20
15–20	Tag it						Vocab review	1.21
35–40	Textbook writers						Writing and speaking around a topic	1.22
10	Texting						Vocab review	1.23
30–40			Too many cooks				Vocab for food, cooking, and recipes	1.24
25–35					Why?		Discussing Art	1.25

Section 2 Sound and video-based activities

Lesson time	Beginner	Elementary	Pre-int	Int	Upper-int	Advanced	Focus	Activity number
15–20		A stroll in the city					Giving directions	2.1
30–40				Advertising slogans			Critical thinking; language of advertising	2.2
15–25	Bingo						Vocab for food	2.3
15–25	Bugging fly						Vocab for furniture and household objects; prep of place	2.4
10–15	Clear your throats						Reading aloud	2.5

Teacher's quick-reference guide

Lesson time	Beginner	Elementary	Pre-int	Int	Upper-int	Advanced	Focus	Activity number
10–15	Countable or uncountable?						Dictation: countable and uncountable nouns	2.6
15–20				Fragmented listening			3rd conditional	2.7
20–30			Get it?				Expressions with *get*	2.8
15–20		Guest speaker					Listening practice	2.9
15–20	How do you say it?						Pron: individual words	2.10
30–40				It's all in the news			Listening to and writing news stories	2.11
10–15	Lips don't lie						Pron: minimal pairs	2.12
Day 1 10–15 Day 2 15–20		Literal video version					Writing texts to match moving images	2.13
Day 1 20–25 Day 2 10–15 Day 3 10–15			Making comics				Giving advice / making suggestions	2.14
5–10	Minimal pairs						Pron: minimal pairs	2.15
20–30				News leak			Writing news stories from key vocab	2.16
10–15	One word at a time						Language chunks	2.17
30–40				Phone messages			Reported speech	2.18
15–20				Put the headphones on			Listening practice	2.19
20–25		Questions for a video clip					Writing questions	2.20
35–45	Ready for test						Speaking test practice	2.21
20–25				Remember			Expressions with *give*	2.22
20–25		Song to sing					Listening practice	2.23
40–60	Sound clips						Writing narratves	2.24

Lesson time	Beginner	Elementary	Pre-int	Int	Upper-int	Advanced	Focus	Activity number
20–25				Speaking exchange			Speaking practice; listening practice	2.25
30–40	The friendliest voice						Analysing poken discourse	2.26
35–45				Translation exchange			Written translation	2.27
15–25	True/False						Listening practice	2.28
20–40						Video board game	Listening practice	2.29
20–25	Voice artists						Pron	2.30

Section 3 Text-based activities								
20–30	A moment in time						Recalling written texts	3.1
10–15	Actions and locations						Present continuous	3.2
Day 1 10–15 Day 2 20–25 Day 3 10–15	Bilingual blog						Writing blog entries	3.3
15–20				British English or American English?			British English vs American English	3.4
10–20			Categories				Vocab review	3.5
8–10 per word		Delving deeper					Word combinations	3.6
25–40			Dreams				Interpreting dreams	3.7
30–50						Find someone who …	Strong collocations	3.8
20–25		Googling for numbers					Numbers, jobs	3.9
10–15				Happiness is …			Listening practice; dictation	3.10
20–30						Health and illness	Health and illness	3.11
20–25		*Luckily/ Unluckily*					Contrasting statements	3.12

Teacher's quick-reference guide

Lesson time	Beginner	Elementary	Pre-int	Int	Upper-int	Advanced	Focus	Activity number
30–40			*Make* or *do*?				Expressions with *make* and *do*	3.13
15–20			Mistake detectives				Correcting grammar and vocab errors	3.14
20–25				Newsflash			Recalling texts; Text editing	3.15
25–30		Present perfect and past simple					Present perfect and past simple; speaking practice	3.16
10–15		Rhyming dictionaries					Pron: vowels	3.17
Chat: 15–20 Correction				Right a wrong			Correcting grammar and vocab errors	3.18
20–30					Sound it		Vocab for sounds	3.19
10–15	Shuffled letters						Vocab review	3.20
10–20			Teleprompter				Reading aloud	3.21
Day 1 30–40 Day 2 15–20				The missing verb			Phrasal verbs	3.22
10–20	Trending topicss						microreading	3.23
10–15					Vague language		Vague language	3.24
10–15	Wikidictionary						Vocab review	3.25
5–10	Wrapping things up						Vocab review	3.26

Credits for pictures

The publishers would like to thank the following for their kind permission to reproduce the following photographs and other copyright material:

ActivInspire p87, p100, p193; **Daniel Martin** p44, p69, p91, p110, p115, p120; Nikanovak p52, Brett Critchley p77 (mall), Absente p77 (restaurant), Warren Rosenberg p77 (library), Libux77 p77 (smartphone), p87 (Millenium Bridge), Luciano Mortula p87 (Tate Modern) | **Dreamstime.com**; **http://en.wiktionary.org** p200; **http://ourbilingualblog.wordpress.com** p154; **http://padlet. com** p173; **http://rhymebrain.com** p183; **https://twitter.com** pp196, p198; ©**iStockphoto.com**/ bowdenimages p77 (office), Paolo Scarlata p77 (cinema), amriphoto p77 (university), Birute p77 (beach), Grafissimo p77 (traffic); **Soledad Palacios** p92; Stephen Finn p87 (House of Parliament), p87 (Buckingham Palace), Tupungato p87 (Covent Garden), David Hughes p87 (Globe), Arvind Balaraman p87 (London Eye), Nicemonkey p72, p106, p115, p144, p146, p158, p160, p164, p167, p173, p179, p183, p196, p198 (browser frame) /**Shutterstock.com**; **Wikimedia Commons** p48, p62; **www.bbc.com** p179; **www.chindogu.com** p37; **www.easyprompter.com** p191; **www.flickr.com**/photos/kyletaylor p34; **www.google.com** p72, p167; **www.google.com**/maps p87; **www.hasbro.com** p158; **www.howysay.com** p106, p115; **www.neatchat.com** p160; **www.netspeak.org** p160; **www.wordle.net** p63, p148, p202; **www.tubechop.com** p144; **www.youtube.com** p146.

As far as our knowledge, all information is correct, on going to press. Every effort has been made to trace the owners of any copyright material in this book. If notified, the publisher will be pleased to rectify any errors or omissions.